LOSING ZOIE

LOSING ZOIE

A mothers heart-breaking story of losing her 14-year-old daughter in a tragic school bus accident

KARINA ADAMS

Contents

Acknowledgements		1
Prologue		2
1	YOUNG ZOIE	4
2	THAT DAY	11
diary		18
3	SHOCK	20
4	THE FIRST TWO WEEKS	26
5	THE FUNERAL	32
diary		36
6	REMINDERS	37
7	NOT COPING	43
8	COUNSELLING AND MEDIUMS	47
9	GRIEF	52
diary		59
10	HOW TO HELP A BEREAVED PARENT	61
11	SUPPORTING THE KIDS WHILE GRIEVING	66
12	SPECIAL OCCASIONS AND DATES	73

diary   76

   13   ZOIE'S ROOM   78
   14   ZOIE'S BIRTHDAY   81
diary   83
   15   GOING BACK TO WORK   85
diary   91
   16   THE COURT CASE   93
   17   HOW I'VE CHANGED   100
   18   1 YEAR ANNIVERSARY   103
   19   OPENING UP   107
   20   DREAMS OF ZOIE   110
   21   MOVING ON   113
diary   116
   22   LIFE WITHOUT ZOIE   118
notes   123
ABOUT THE AUTHOR   129

Copyright © 2022 by Karina Adams

All rights reserved. No part of this book may be reproduced in any manner whatsoever without written permission except in the case of brief quotations embodied in critical articles and reviews.

First Printing, 2022

Acknowledgements

To my husband, Aaron, you are my comfort, my rock, my calm in the eye of the storm.

To my four sons, Jacob, Tyson, Charlie and Riley, you were my light in the dark and kept me pushing for a better tomorrow.

To my immediate and extended family, thank you for your unconditional love and support.

To my daughter, Zoie, I miss you beyond measure every day. Your life was a blessing.

To my editor, Giselle Alegria, thank you for taking the time to read over my manuscript and for your honest opinion and corrections.

To the whole Ulladulla community, thank you from the bottom of my heart for your generosity, love and support.

The content in this book is my opinion and my personal truth. Some names have been changed to protect their identities.

Prologue

When my daughter, Zoie, died, my whole world, as I knew it, fell apart. I had to learn how to live again when I really didn't want to. I felt lost. I felt that my family and I were all alone and I couldn't get real-life stories and information about what I was going through. I needed to know if there was a way to survive this horrendous pain.

There are many books on grief, but I struggled to find any true stories on child loss. I wasn't interested in reading a book written by a professional, who had not felt my emptiness and heartache, offering helpful tips from a textbook to manage grief. I didn't believe there was a way for me to get better, so I wanted to know how other bereaved parents survived the tragedy of losing their child, how they felt and what they went through. I guess I just wanted my desolation acknowledged. I wanted to know that there was someone else who fully understood what I was going through. That is what I hope others will get from this book.

I needed to know that I was not alone. That everything I was thinking and feeling was normal. I needed to know if life could ever be bearable again

It is every parent's worst fear to have one of their children die before them, but no one ever truly believes that it will actually happen.

When the unthinkable did actually happen, I didn't believe it for weeks. Being told that my only daughter had been hit by a bus and died was like something out of a movie. It was impossible to process. For months afterwards, I would tell myself that Zoie was just living overseas or on a long holiday, and that she would be back, because I just couldn't accept that she was gone.

I hit the lowest of lows that I had ever felt. I was numb. Living in a dark fog. I thought it couldn't possibly get any worse. Then I got to a point where I thought I was coming good. The days got a little easier. I cried less each day. Then I sank even lower again. I used every ounce of energy I had just to breathe. I see and hear everything differently now. Figuring out how to love life again, without my daughter, is the longest and hardest thing I have ever had to do. I don't believe I will ever fully recover from that life shattering tragedy, but the days do get easier. If you are a newly bereaved parent, you have a massive challenge ahead of you and there is no easy way to get through it. There is no magic cure. It is just something you must do for as long as it takes. You have a long, dark road ahead of you. It won't be easy, but it can be done. It won't be a happy, triumphant victory at the end, just mere survival. I am living proof of that. This is the story of what I went through after losing my 14year-old daughter, Zoie, in a school bus accident.

I

YOUNG ZOIE

Mum and I have always had a close relationship. She knew I wasn't happy and having relationship issues, so she and Noel cut their trip around Australia short to be with me when I had my baby. Mum and Noel were staying in a caravan park nearby in Tallebudgera on the Gold Coast in Queensland. They were to move into a unit on Saturday, 25 March.

One week before Zoie was born, I left her father, Nathan (for the first time), to stay with mum in the caravan. The timing was good, in a way, because Noel was away for a couple of weeks for work. With only the one bed in the caravan, mum and I shared it. I spent those few days relaxing in the Gold Coast sun. After a year of being unhappy, I felt relaxed, like I was on a holiday. The only downside was having to walk about 100 meters, in the middle of the night, to the toilets. I would roll out of bed as quietly as I could manage and waddle through the park with my huge pregnant belly leading the way.

It was four days before Zoie was due and I was in complete denial that I was in labour. I continued to go shopping with mum for the day and kept complaining that I had a pain in my stomach.

'Are you in labour?' mum asked me.

'No. It's not that bad', I replied, 'I just need some Panadol and a lie down'. Well, the Panadol didn't work and the pain got worse.

'I think I better take you to the hospital, just to check you out', mum said.

So, at about 3pm, I got my prepacked hospital bag and mum drove me to the hospital. By the time I got there, was given a bed and the nurse had checked me over, I was 9 cm dilated. Zoie was born on Friday, 24 March, 2006 at 10:21pm. She was born with a full head of dark brown hair and had the brightest blue eyes.

Zoie was the perfect baby. She slept right through the night from eight weeks old and never cried; just gave a little grizzle when she was hungry. Zoie was a bright and smart child. In preschool, she knew all her colours, numbers, the alphabet and could spell her name.

I went on to have two more children with Nathan (Jacob and Tyson) before I left him for the third and final time. Zoie loved and adored her younger brothers. Zoie was like my shadow, always helping me with the boys and she became a little mum to them, sometimes getting a bit too bossy and I would have to remind her who the mum was.

I was a single mum of three, living in my hometown of Ulladulla, NSW, when I met Aaron. Zoie was 5, Jacob was three and Tyson was 11 months old. Aaron was great with them and bonded with all three instantly. Aaron and I were inseparable from the start. He has always been my rock. We just connected on every level. We share all the same family values. We have all the same interests and we want the same lifestyle. I had finally found the Prince Charming I had always dreamed about and thought was just a fairy tale. Aaron was slightly taller than I, had short dark hair and dreamy blue eyes that would sparkle when he looked at me. He often surprised me with a bunch of flowers and treated me like a princess. We shared the same dream of one day owning our own home and travelling around Australia later during our retirement. I honestly believe that Aaron and I are soul mates, like our souls were connected and we finally found each other again here on Earth.

Six months later, we were living together, got engaged and married two years later. Aaron has two children from a previous marriage, Charlie (5) and Riley (3). Six months after Aaron moved in with me, Charlie and Riley moved in with us too, as their mother was moving to live in Sydney, three hours away. She would be working full time and would have no family up there to help with the kids. Aaron and I felt that not getting to see them often was not an option, so it was a no brainer that the boys should live with us. So, just like that, my family of five became a family of 7.

We are an open and honest family. I like to encourage the kids to talk to us about anything, from school, friends, our family, sex, drugs; anything. As long as they are honest and respectful, they can say anything at the dinner table, without consequences. We tell of our highs and lows of each day. It's a great way to get the kids to talk about their day. I often got asked what my biggest fear was, and I would always respond with, 'Losing one of my children'. And it was. It is every parent's worst fear to lose a child, but I felt deep in my soul that one day this would become a reality for me. I would randomly worry about it often and it would bring me to tears.

Zoie was an active, fun-loving girl. She loved our family camping trips. We would often go camping at Yadboro, which is a beautiful open camping ground by a freshwater river, about 20 kms into the bush. There was no power, phone service or facilities. There was just nature. I have been camping there since I was a toddler, with my family. My brothers and I have continued that tradition with our own kids. Zoie and her brothers would go out and play and explore, often jumping off a rock into the river. One of their favorite things to do was riding in the back of the Ute. The kids would stand on the back, always in the same spot, holding on as Aaron would drive them up the dirt road.

Zoie was never a sporty person, but she loved physie, dance and gymnastics. Zoie started physie when she was 5. I really enjoyed the physie days and I believe Zoie did too. Zoie competed in a few physie competitions. I would curl her hair and do her make up beforehand. She made it to zone once, placing in the top five. Physie was our mother daughter time. Zoie is my only daughter. With four loud, rough boys at home, I cherished our girly times.

At about the age of 10, Zoie changed to hip hop dance. She was a little uncoordinated at first, but soon picked it up.

Zoie had only participated in dance for a short while before she changed to gymnastics at about the age of 12. Here, she was in her element. It wasn't so serious. There were no competitions. She could just go, have a bit of fun jumping and flipping around.

After years of being a mostly stay-at-home mum, in 2018, I started working part-time in aged care. I loved it and finally felt that I had found my calling. Soon after I started working there, I had two skin cancers removed from my face. A few months later, I found out I had breast cancer and had to have a lumpectomy and six weeks of radiotherapy. I continued to work throughout my treatment. Several other staff members have had something bad happen to them, like the death of a child or partner or cancer. I would always joke that the place was cursed, but still I continued to work there.

Teenage Zoie

Zoie was my soul child. She and I were connected on a deep, spiritual level. We would really get each other's jokes. We would know each other's thoughts with just a look. She was so smart, witty and had a sarcastic sense of humour. Zoie didn't care what others thought of her. She was internal with her feelings. She would get quiet sometimes and I'd know she had something on her mind. Most of the time, I didn't even have to ask her; I would just know what was bugging her.

The teenage years are my favorite. I only got two of those years with Zoie. She had long, naturally blonde hair and her blue eyes had changed to green.

She had grown into a beautiful, kind, sensible, wise and considerate young lady.

Zoie was independent, stubborn and would stand up for what she believed in. Zoie was full of charisma.

She would light up a room as soon as she walked in, but in a quiet, subtle way. She was known to walk into class quietly singing nursery rhymes to herself. Zoie would often walk in the door after school and call out, 'Hi. Can I have food? Thanks!'

Zoie was a loyal friend. She accepted and loved people for who they were, without judgement or expectation.

Zoie was intelligent but played dumb. She would often make fun of herself for being clumsy and a bit of a ditz. Zoie loved life. Zoie was a beautiful soul who always seemed to be smiling and laughing. She's the girl that no one who met her will ever forget.

2020 was tough from the start. Little did I know that it was going to be the toughest time of my life. We started the year off with the Currowan Fire, which burned for 74 days across 499,621 hectares of the Shoalhaven, destroying 312 homes. It wasn't a normal summer holiday, spending time at the beach with friends and family. We ended up spending our holidays indoors, as there was smoke and ash everywhere. We couldn't go camping or leave town because the whole town was surrounded by bush and was on fire. Then COVID-19 hit. The five kids were all home schooled. I had to cut down on my hours at work. It was just too much to be a teacher all morning and go to work each afternoon. I was exhausted.

I was so proud of Zoie. She just took this new chapter of life in her stride. Covid and home schooling didn't really bother her. She would get herself ready for a morning of schoolwork, never needing any help from me. Zoie's friends were a big part of her life. Not even Covid could stop that. Zoie had the best group of friends. They are all so caring and supportive of each other.

Zoie would speak with her girlfriends in video chats on the laptop all day. They would chat and help each other with their schoolwork, often while joking and laughing. Zoie even sat her laptop on the kitchen bench one day, talking with the girls while she baked a chocolate cake. It was like I had Zoie's friends here every day.

The kids all gradually returned to school in Term 2. Life was starting to feel a little normal again. The boys were happy to be back at school and see all their mates again, and I could pick up a little more work.

Aaron and I decided that we would pay off our debts as quickly as we could and begin saving a deposit for a home. We started getting excited and looking at houses and properties. I woke Zoie one morning and asked her if she wanted to come with me to look at display homes. I didn't think she would be all that interested. She instantly sat up, with excitement in her eyes and a big smile and said, 'Yes!'

She was so excited about the possibility of getting our own home. Zoie paced through each house, excitedly picking out which would be her room in each one. I told her to lie in the bathtubs, so I could see if they were big enough. She looked at me with doubt, like, are you crazy? but did so anyway with a cheeky giggle, like she was doing something wrong.

About a week before Zoie died, I had not long gone to bed and was just about to sleep when I got this strange feeling of a negative energy next to my bed. It told me, in a thought more than actual words, that it was coming for one of my family members. That their time was up. I didn't fear this energy. I didn't feel as though it was going to do any harm. It was just a warning or message of some kind. I remember replying, in my mind, 'No. You're not having any of us. Leave us alone'.

Now, I believe in spirits and the spiritual world, but I don't believe in ghosts or demons or anything like that. At the time, I just thought, Shit, I'm going crazy. I must just be tired. I soon fell asleep and forgot all about it.

2

THAT DAY

Wednesday, 1 July started like any other Wednesday. It was two days away from the winter school holidays. Aaron and I both had the day off. I got up and showered and went and opened Zoie's bedroom door for her usual morning wake-up call.

'Good morning, wakey, wakey. Time to get up'.

I then did the same with the four boys and packed their school lunches.

Zoie was dressed in her grey school pants and light grey Everlast hoodie. She lived in that bloody hoodie. I could not for the life of me get her to wear her school jumper.

At 8:30 am, we all got into the car and dropped Zoie and Charlie at school. We pulled up at the side of Ulladulla High School, just down from the corner of St Vincent and South Streets. That bloody corner.

'Love you. Have a good day. Bye', I called out from the front seat as they got out of the car.

'Love you too. Bye', Zoie replied. They were the last words I heard Zoie say.

We continued to drop the younger three boys at the primary school. Aaron and I did our grocery shopping, came home and put all the shopping away. I then went out to meet my girlfriends, Shelly and Loren, for a coffee in town just around the corner from the high school.

At about 3.10pm, Loren's partner, Shane, called her and said that he was parked and waiting at the school to pick up their son, that there had been an accident and it looked like someone had been hit.

Suddenly there were sirens. Several police cars and ambulance came speeding past, one after the other. I instantly thought of Zoie and got a horrible, gut-wrenching feeling. I said to the girls, 'Zoie and Charlie cross the road up there to walk home. I better call them'. I called Zoie's phone. No answer. That's strange, I thought. It's after school, so she would have had her phone on her. I called again... Twice. Still no answer. I then called Charlie at 3:20 pm. Charlie answered. He was home, but Zoie was not. 'Tell Zoie to call me as soon as she gets home', I told him.

I called Zoie again. No answer. I messaged her, saying 'Call me ASAP'. By this time, I knew deep down that it was Zoie. It was not like her not to answer her phone. Zoie would always call me during the day if she wanted to go to the shop or Maccas after school. She even called me from a friend's phone sometimes if she didn't have her phone or had no credit.

'Something is wrong', I told the girls. 'I have to go find Zoie'.

I got back to my car and called Aaron. He was picking up the younger three boys from the primary school. 'Can you call me when you get home and let me know if Zoie is home? There has been an accident at the high school, and I can't get a hold of her', I said.

I started to panic. I had been having coffee maybe 200 metres around the corner from the accident.

For whatever reason, I couldn't walk there to check. Instead, I drove all over town, avoiding the accident, to look for Zoie. I drove to McDonald's. Walked inside. No Zoie.

Shelly called me as I was driving towards Coles. 'It's bad', she said. I just drove past the accident and there is a blue sheet over a body lying on the road.'

I got to Coles. Tears were running down my face. There was no sign of Zoie in Coles. I walked up the street towards Woolworths. Aaron called me before I got there.

'Hey, can you come home?', he asked.

I could here in his voice that something was terribly wrong.

'Is Zoie home?' I asked.

'No, just come home', he replied.

'Bad news?' I asked.

'Yeah, a little bit', Aaron said, through a sob, after hesitating. He didn't want to ever hurt me and now he had to tell me the worst thing a parent could hear. He didn't want to be the one to tell me the news that was going to hurt me more than anything. "Ok, I'm on my way", I replied.

Panic set in. My world started to crumble. I ran back to my car and drove home five minutes around the corner. There was school traffic and children were everywhere. There were police cars blocking my usual roads home. Shit. Move out of my way. How do I get home? I thought. I had to go the long way around.

I had to stop at a roundabout as more police cars sped past in front of me with lights and sirens on, towards the accident.

Shelly called for an update on Zoie. I told her about my conversation with Aaron and that I was on my way home.

'I'm turning around', she said. 'I'll be there in a minute'.

Oh Fuck. No. Not my Zoie. Please let her be okay. Maybe she just witnessed the accident and is traumatised. We can deal with that. Maybe it was one of her friends. Oh no, not one of the girls.

I pulled into my street, and I could see a blue and white police car parked out the front of my house. Aaron was standing on the driveway with two police officers. No Zoie. As I parked the car on my front lawn, a wave of emotion painfully crushed my chest and I struggled to breathe. No. No. No. Not Zoie. My head fell forward onto the stirring wheel. Aaron opened my door, turned the car off and held me as he helped me out of the car. The two policeman walked towards me slowly with their heads hung low and 'that' look on their faces. That look of sadness and empathy. My legs were weak beneath me. I still couldn't breathe. I felt like I was drowning.

'I'm sorry', one of the policemen said.

'No, no, no', I said, sobbing and fell to the ground. Aaron helped me up and led me to the house. I only made it to the front steps and had to sit down. Shock set in and I was uncontrollably shaking all over.

I don't remember the exact words, but the policemen continued to tell me that Zoie was hit by a school bus and had died at the scene.

'A fucking bus', I spat out the words in shock and horror. Oh, my baby had no chance.

My mind went blank. I felt lost. I didn't know what needed to be done. I'd never experienced a death of a close family member. I had never organised a funeral.

'What do I do now? Do I need to go to ID her body?' I asked. The policemen told me that Zoie's body will be taken to the hospital morgue and that I needed to contact the funeral director, who would handle everything from there.

They asked me if there was anyone I needed them to contact for me. Again, I was blank, but at the same time, my mind was running. My first thought was mum. I needed to call mum. She can call the rest of the family for me. Then it occurred to me that I needed to tell Zoie's dad. Oh no, I can't do that over the phone, I thought, and I'm not leaving this house.

"Yes, Zoie's dad", I replied. "He is on his own and lives in Batemans Bay!"

I gave the police officer Nathan's address and phone number and they organised for the Batemans Bay police officers to go to his house and tell him. And that was that. They were gone. We were left there, lost, in shock, in denial, still waiting for Zoie to come walking up the road.

The news spread so fast. I'd had calls and messages of condolences coming in while I was still talking with the policemen.

I called mum and Noel and asked them to come over. I just couldn't tell them over the phone.

'Can you both come over to the house?' was all I could get out. Noel must have heard in my voice that something was seriously wrong.

'Ok, be there soon', he replied.

I was still sitting on the front step, Aaron sitting behind me, holding me. We were both crying when mum and Noel showed up 15 minutes later.

Mum dropped to her knees in front of me and hugged me.

'What's happened?' she asked.

I couldn't get any words out, so Aaron answered for me.

'It's Zoie. She's not coming home', he replied. He couldn't say the words either.

'What do you mean that Zoie's not coming home?' mum asked, as tears started rolling down her face.

'She died', I sobbed. Somehow, I managed to tell her what had happened.

Oh shit, the boys. Where are the boys? I need to tell the boys. How do I tell them something like this? They were all inside. Aaron had sent them in when he saw the police car pull up out front. God only knows what would have been going through their minds. Had they been watching through the window? Did they have any idea what was happening? I gathered them all together at the dining table. I knew I had to be honest and direct. This was shit. There was no way to sugar coat it and I didn't want the boys to hear any information about the accident from friends. It had to be from me. I hugged them all. I cried. I then took a deep breath and said, "I have bad news, boys. Zoie's been in an accident. She was hit by a bus while walking home from school and she died".

By this time, we had my parents, my brother, and my four close friends from school, Shelly, Loren, Rachele and Jenna, at my house. I have no idea how they all knew. I assume they all contacted each other to spread the news because I don't remember calling anyone, apart from mum. I had long-distance friends and family call within hours and arriving at my house within days. That's just how close we all are. Everyone we knew was there to support us instantly.

They ordered pizza for the boys for dinner. Aaron and I couldn't eat anything. I was now numb. It was like being stuck in a thick fog. I wasn't aware of anyone around me. I felt like I was drowning. There was a crushing feeling in my chest. All I could do was sit in my chair on the front verandah and try to breathe. It was so hard to breathe. We could hear siren after siren all evening, because the accident was only 1 km away from our home. Shut up. Stop. I just wanted the sirens to stop.

We didn't want to be away from the boys that night, so we pulled out the camp mattresses. Aaron, the four boys and I all slept in the lounge room together. Aaron and I didn't sleep though. I could hear the boys sniffling and wiping their tears away as they cried but tried to hide it. It broke my heart to hear them so upset, knowing that I couldn't take their pain away. All I could do was hug them as I cried with them. I was hurting so bad myself. My chest was tight. I couldn't breathe. I was irritable. I wanted to comfort my boys, but I also wanted to be alone with Aaron. I lay there tossing and turning for hours. Thoughts were rolling through my head. Someone please tell me this is all a nightmare. A sick joke. Shit like this doesn't happen to us. Maybe there had been a mistake. Maybe it wasn't Zoie. Zoie, please come home. Aaron and I lay there crying until about 3 am before we just gave up on sleeping. We got up and had a cuppa.

The boys built forts in the lounge room and slept in them each night for the first two weeks. It was school holidays and I think it gave them comfort to all be together.

diary

Thurs, 2/7/2020

Dear diary,
No sleep last night.
I am so tired. I feel so drained, but I can't sleep. My mind won't stop. Every time I close my eyes, I see Zoie. I am numb and in disbelief. I just can't believe Zoie died yesterday. Shit like this doesn't happen to our family. I cry myself to sleep each night and cry the moment I wake, usually two hours later. My days are spent sitting in my chair on the front verandah with Aaron and our family and friends, who pop in and out all day. I have cuppa after cuppa, numbly watching this one Willy Wag Tail that comes and goes, dancing around at the top of my driveway. It's strange because I don't remember seeing it before.

~

A reporter from 10 News came to my house asking if I wanted to say anything. Yeah right, as if I'm going to tell my story on TV less than 24 hours after my daughter died. I can't even put a whole sentence together, dick head.
How fucking rude to turn up at my house. I'm sure you
could find a shit load of people around the accident site at 3 pm. Get that road on TV at 3 pm and maybe the council and NSW roads and transport will realise how busy it is.

~

The police came by to give me Zoie's belongings from her school bag. I had to describe Zoie, her height and what she had been wearing. I also had to identify Zoie's bag from a photo, zoomed in on just the pattern, not the whole bag! Everything except her laptop was completely shattered. How was her laptop the only thing not damaged? Why don't I get her bag back too? I didn't even ask. It's probably covered in her blood.

~

Did she see the bus coming? Was she scared? Was she in pain? Or did she not see it coming and she was gone before she knew what had happened. Oh, I hope it was quick.

I wish I could have been there. Maybe I could have helped her. Maybe I could have stopped her crossing at that moment.

Rach and Shelly set up a 'go fund me' page. We said no at first. We don't want handouts. But eventually, they talked me into it because they were right. We would be screwed without an income, and I have no idea how long we will have off work. We thought, even if we just get a couple thousand dollars, it will help us for a couple of weeks. We were completely overwhelmed when it reached $4,000 in half an hour.

Oh my God. We have such an amazing community.

How will I ever thank them?

3

SHOCK

For the first few weeks, I was frozen with shock. My whole body felt numb. I had a million thoughts continually running through my head, yet my mind was blank. I couldn't process what I wanted or needed to do. I had no urge to make conversation with anyone. I didn't even think to eat unless someone gave me something and told me to eat it.

Aaron and I would just sit on our front verandah every day in the winter sun. I couldn't do anything but breathe and sitting out in the sun helped calm me and clear my head. We had all our friends and family over. They would talk amongst themselves and make cups of tea. I would sit and watch this one Willy Wag Tail bird. It would come each day and sit on a post at the top of my driveway, look at me, wag its tail around for a moment and then fly away. That's strange, I thought. In the six years we'd been living here, I don't remember ever seeing a Willy Wag Tail bird around my house.

I took it as a sign of some sort from Zoie. Maybe she was just letting me know that she was still around.

I couldn't string more than a few words together. And I had a million horrific thoughts rolling through my head. How? Did she not look? No, of course she would have looked. She knows how busy that road is. She's been crossing at that same spot for three years! Was she on her phone? Did she hit the bus and bounce off? Did she go under the wheels? What is her body like? Could I even ID her? And then the wave would hit me again and again. Pulling me under. Drowning me. Breathe. Just breathe, I'd tell myself.

We had a reporter from 10 news come to the house asking if we wanted to say anything about our loss. How fucking rude, I thought. How dare you come to my home when I'm privately grieving. My daughter just died yesterday. Not even 24 hours ago. I'm a mess. I can't put two words together and you want me to tell my story on TV. You have got to be fucking kidding. He did get his story though, from members of the community, the school and two of my friends, who asked my permission first. I thought it was going to be big news in our small town and I preferred that my close friends tell the facts for me, rather than the media just getting gossip. It was on the local news on the Thursday night. We all sat together, crying in the lounge room and watched the news as they told the story of a 14year-old, Ulladulla High School student dying after being hit by a school bus. They mentioned Zoie's name and had photos of her from social media. It was so surreal. I was still in disbelief. This could not be my daughter. We are just regular people. We don't have stuff like this happen to us. We don't appear on the news.

For the first week, our home was open to all. We constantly had friends, family and police detectives come and go. Two new policemen came around to give me a large brown paper bag containing Zoie's belongings from her school bag. I never did get her school bag back and I never asked why. I just presumed that it was covered in her blood. There was a big dent in her deodorant can. Her pens and pencils were shattered. Her school calculator was smashed. And her laptop, her new laptop with a hard protective case, still looked new. There was only one small scratch on it and it still worked perfectly. In fact, Zoie's laptop is what I'm using to write this book on. I couldn't believe it. Zoie's laptop was the only thing to survive the accident. It was a sign. I had to do something meaningful with it. I had to tell my story.

I'd had to describe to the police officer over the phone what Zoie was wearing, her appearance, height, etc. Sometime later, the officer came to the house and asked me to ID Zoie's school bag. He showed me a close-up photo on his phone of a pink floral print. It was not the whole bag, just a section of it. "Yes, that's Zoie's bag" I said with a lump in my throat.

I was then asked to give them Zoie's hairbrush and toothbrush for identification purposes. I froze. Oh, my baby girl. She's a mess. No wonder they wouldn't let me go see her body. At that stage, I still had not been into Zoie's room. It was too painful to not see her lying on her bed. Aaron quickly beat me to it, getting Zoie's hairbrush and toothbrush from her room. He wanted to save me the pain and torment.

The night after Zoie died, at 3 am, I was lying in bed, trying and failing to sleep. I was crying and staring at the wall and that's when I saw her. I saw a vision of Zoie on the wall. It was like a 3D hologram light. Zoie was lying on her side with her arm under her head. She just smiled at me. Then, as a thought more than actual words, I heard her say, Hey, I'm okay. I'm with nan and pop. They are pretty cool'. I got the feeling that she was telling me that she was happy and liked it in heaven. It only lasted a minute and then she was gone.

I thought I must be going crazy. Maybe I was delusional because I hadn't slept. Whatever it was, I wanted it back. I wanted to see and talk to my daughter again. Aaron was not in the bed. I went to find him and found him on the front veranda.

'The weirdest thing just happened', he said. 'I think I just saw Zoie standing on the back of the Ute, like she did when we were camping!' 'Was it a light, like a hologram?' I asked.

'Yes', he replied.

I explained what I had seen on the wall. We had experienced the same thing. Seeing Zoie calmed me, and I was able to get two hours of sleep. We never saw her again.

The house resembled a florist for weeks. Every day we had several deliveries of flowers. We had so much love and support from the whole community. It was overwhelming. Our neighbour made us a lasagne. We had people drop off boxes and boxes of cooked meals in containers, ready to freeze and reheat and all kinds of snacks for the kids. It was amazing and so helpful. We could just be with each other and grieve and I didn't have to worry about cooking. The kids could just heat something up. Aaron's work mates showed up with a car boot full of groceries for us. Meat, vegetables, fruit, milk, juice, milo, biscuits. We were sorted for weeks. It was so appreciated and helped more than they could imagine. The only thing they forgot was alcohol, so we ordered it from Woolworths online. We couldn't bring ourselves to go into town. We didn't want to leave the house. In a weird way, I felt closer to Zoie at home. I could feel her spirit at home, especially in her room. I just wanted to stay at home and be close to my girl.

The thought of being seen in town and judged for being out and about, or running into someone I knew and having to talk to them, was debilitating.

The high school was supportive and kept in contact with me. The students all wrote notes and letters and made paper cranes. There was a memorial of flowers and teddies left at the school fence.

On the Friday after Zoie's accident, Aaron drove us to the school to see the memorial of flowers. It was a long and harrowing five-minute drive. Aaron and I were so nervous driving for a long time afterwards, especially at intersections or whenever we saw pedestrians. We couldn't bring ourselves to drive past that corner. We chose to drive on the back roads to the school. As we pulled up and parked at the front of the school, I could see that corner. The image of my Zoie lying on the road was in my head. The wave was building again. Crushing my chest.

I couldn't breathe. I started hyperventilating. I lay my head forward in my hands and cried. Pull yourself together Karina, I told myself. With Aarons arm around me and holding onto the boys, we slowly made our way into the school. My legs were shaking. All our friends and family were waiting at the front of the school for us.

I brought the teddies and the two boxes of letters and paper cranes home. Aaron and I read through every note and letter. There were hundreds of them. Some were from close friends of Zoie's. Others were from people that didn't know Zoie personally but wanted to send their condolences anyway. Some said that they were not close to Zoie, but that she had always been nice to them and brightened up their every day at school. They were all so beautiful and highlighted just how kind and caring Zoie was, how loved and how much she meant to all those people. What's sad about it is that I don't think Zoie had any idea the impact she had on the world around her. Zoie was just being Zoie. Living in the moment. Living every day to the fullest. Zoie was known for being kind to everyone. She didn't pick sides when her friends would fight. As Zoie's friends started to separate into different groups, Zoie couldn't choose just one group, so she bounced around all her friends. She was a loyal and supportive friend.

All I ever hoped for from my parenting was that my children were always kind, polite and respectful, so it filled my heart with pride when the mother of one of Zoie's friends called me in the weeks following Zoie's death to thank me for raising such a kind-hearted daughter. She told me of a time when her daughter was crying in the school toilets after being bullied. This girl had been so upset and her spirit was broken. She felt all alone and there was no end to her torment. Zoie sat with her and listened, comforted her and wouldn't leave her until she was ready to face the day again, with Zoie by her side.

4

THE FIRST TWO WEEKS

For the first week, I didn't sleep more than two or three hours each night. I could not stop crying for more than half an hour. I cried all day. Every day. I remember thinking, surely, I can't have any more tears left to cry, but they just kept falling. I had to apply a face cream several times a day because the skin around my eyes was red, sore and cracking from crying and wiping my eyes so often.

After a week, I decided it was time I started to cook so that we had dinner at the table all together again. I needed some sort of normality back. Dinner time was when Zoie would come and hang out in the kitchen with me while I cooked. I would be preparing the food on the middle island kitchen bench while Zoie would be swinging between the island bench and the side bench. We would talk about her day or chat about what was going on with her and her friends. We were close. She could tell me anything. If she ever had something on her mind, I could always tell before she even said anything, just by the look in her eyes or a vibe I would get from her.

Instead of swinging about, Zoie would lean on the bench, looking down like she was deep in thought.

I stood in the kitchen, cutting the vegetables, staring at Zoie's bedroom door in front of me like I was waiting for her to come out and talk to me. I cried, took a sip of my wine and kept going. You can do this Karina, I'd tell myself. The family still need to eat.

I sat staring at Zoie's empty seat next to me at the dinner table. Tears start rolling down my face again. 'Mum, you have been crying for a week straight', Tyson said.

'Yes, buddy I have'.

'Your worst nightmare came true', he said. That broke me. The wave was back, dragging me down. Drowning me. Breathe Karina, just breathe.

Dinner times were hard for a long time. Aaron and I started to drink more than usual. Most nights, it was only one or two drinks, but it was every night. It helped calm me and got me through each evening.

The boys don't say how they are feeling. How can they? I don't know how to express how I feel. How could school age children process their feelings? I would tell the boys when I was feeling sad and struggling. I would tell them that it's okay to be sad. To cry. To be angry. I wanted them to know that everything they were feeling was normal. It hurts. It is shit, but you're not alone. 'We can all feel shit together', I would tell them.

After four days of lying in the morgue, Zoie was taken to Wollongong forensic pathology for an autopsy. The cause of death was 'multiple injuries (head)'. The picture of Zoie, unrecognisable, stayed in my head for a long, agonising week until Zoie finally went to the Milton Ulladulla funeral directors. Simon and Kathleen were fantastic. They walked us through, step-by-step, the whole process of organising the funeral. Kathleen told me that Zoie was all cleaned up and dressed in the clothes I had provided for her and that, apart from a small cut above Zoie's eye that had been stitched up, she looked rather good. She asked if I wanted to view Zoie's body.

I was in two minds. I wanted to see Zoie so bad. I wanted to hold her and say goodbye. But I didn't want that to be the last image I had of her. I wanted to remember her smile, her laugh and her bright, bubbly and cheeky personality. I decided I was not going to see Zoie's body. Not like that. Not still, cold and emotionless. That's not Zoie. That is just Zoie's body. Her avatar. Zoie is here at home with me. I feel her here with me.

I asked the policemen and the crash investigator many questions for weeks. I needed to know exactly what had happened and how. I just couldn't understand how Zoie was hit. She had crossed at that same spot every day for three years. She was a sensible girl. She was responsible. The police and the crash investigator spoke to many witnesses. They saw dash cam footage from an oncoming car and the video surveillance footage from the bus.

They knew what I needed to know. They were reluctant to tell me all of the details, but I got what I needed from them.

Zoie crossed the road at the corner of St Vincent and South Streets. From the curb, she had looked right for oncoming, northbound traffic. There was a Ute that had stopped at the intersection on South Street and was about to turn left onto St Vincent Street. The bus was behind the Ute. The ute turned left and continued passed Zoie. Zoie then stepped out onto the road thinking that she had a clear path on her side of the road. She looked left for southbound traffic and continued to cross. At the same time, the bus rolled through the stop sign and turned left onto St Vincent Street. Zoie was a few metres away from the curb when the left-hand side of the bus hit her from her right. Zoie hadn't seen it coming. She did not have her phone on her; I found it later that evening in her room, set to silent.

Fri, 3/7/2020

Dear diary,
Two hours sleep last night.
We went to see the tribute of flowers and teddies left at the school fence, and the cranes and letters the students made. It was so overwhelming to see all the love and support. Zoie touched so many people's lives and had no idea. It was so fucking hard to see that corner. I could picture Zoie lying there dead on the road. I couldn't breathe. I felt like I was drowning. I was shaking all over. My legs were weak.

Sat, 4/7/2020

Dear diary,
Today was my 34th birthday, 3 days after Zoie died. There was no cake. No 'happy birthdays' because, obviously, it wasn't going to be a happy one. I had all my closest friends and family come over and they just sat and drank with me, watching the football. I even cracked a smile or two, but then instantly felt like a fraud and felt guilty. And then I'd cry, again.

Sun, 5/7/2020

Dear Diary,
Five hours sleep last night.
I have moved from shock and denial to anger. Think I'll have a day at home tomorrow with limited visitors. I am angry and frustrated all the time. I have little patience with the boys. They are angry and fighting with each other. Why can't they just behave? Oh, my poor babies are hurting too and probably don't understand their feelings. It breaks my heart to see them so sad and angry. I wish I could make them feel better.

Mon, 6/7/2020

Dear diary,
Seven hours sleep last night.
I had a nightmare last night about Zoie being murdered.

I am frustrated that Zoie's body is still not peaceful. My poor baby has been lying in the morgue. Today Zoie was transferred to Wollongong for an autopsy. Cause of death was 'consistent with multiple injuries (head)'. I just want her cleaned up, dressed and resting peacefully.

Feeling strangely calm but still cry several times a day. Boys are cranky, emotional and fighting. I just can't deal with it. My heart breaks all over again because I need to be there for them. I need to be the calm, caring nurturing mother, but I just don't have the energy.

Tues, 7/7/2020

Dear diary,

Three hours sleep last night.

Quiet day today with limited visitors. Mum has been over every day. I don't know if she wants to make sure I'm okay or that she just feels closer to Zoie here.

Picked out Zoie's coffin today. It is beautiful with a picture of a river running through a bush. It reminded us of where we go camping.

Tyson went to the movies with Susanna (his ex-step mum) today. It was good for him to get out. Jacob wanted to stay home.

All boys seem okay emotionally and are starting to voice their emotions. They have built forts in the lounge room and slept in them since Thursday. I think it is comforting for them to stay together.

I cooked our first family meal tonight. I drank my glass of wine, glancing at Zoie's bedroom door, crying as I prepared dinner. We sat at the dinner table all together like we used to. I stared at Zoie's empty seat next to me and cried.

Wed, 8/7/2020

Dear diary,

Woke at 1:30am with a pain in my chest and couldn't go back to sleep. Had to change funeral venue due to bad weather forecast.

Finally, after a long, painful week, my baby is at the funeral home *today. Cleaned up, dressed and in her coffin resting peacefully. I am strangely calm.*

5

THE FUNERAL

Zoie had never had a broken bone. Never had stitches. The thought of how battered Zoie's body must have been was constant torture. I couldn't bring myself to see my baby girl so broken and injured. I hated waiting almost two weeks for Zoie's funeral. Zoie's body was just lying in the morgue for five days, waiting to go to the coroner for an autopsy, to be poked and prodded. Then, finally, two days later, she was taken to the Ulladulla funeral home where she was cleaned up and dressed in her ripped jeans and black Fila hoodie. I decided I didn't want to view Zoie's body. I didn't want to see her cold, injured and emotionless. I wanted to remember her for who she was, happy and smiling.

My sister-in-law, Casie, stayed with the boys while we finalised the funeral details at the funeral home and picked out Zoie's coffin. It was a strange feeling to be walking into a large, cold room with only one door and no windows. All four walls were shelved and full, floor to ceiling, with coffins. There were plain wooden coffins, traditional, morbid brown or white coffins and a beautiful white one with purple butterflies all over it. I couldn't stand the thought of Zoie in a plain, morbid, horrible box. Walking around this room, looking at all the different coffins, I could picture Zoie, mucking around, happily getting inside each one, lying down inside to try it out, like she had done with the bathtubs when we went looking at display homes. 'Nope, not this one', I could hear her saying. We decided on one with a picture of a wide river flowing through the middle of the bush. It looked like the river where we go camping and reminded us of Zoie jumping off the rock into the river. It was beautiful.

We anticipated a large funeral attendance. The whole school community was affected in one way or another by Zoie's death. Everyone was either a close friend of Zoie's, one of her teachers, or had witnessed the accident. The wider community either had children that went to that school and crossed that road too, they had kids who were friends with our boys, or they knew me, Aaron or our extended family.

Because of COVID-19, we had restrictions on the amount of people we could have indoors, so we first decided to have Zoie's funeral at the local football field. We had to change the venue at the last minute to the Dunn Lewis Centre, due to forecasted thunderstorms. We could fit 300 people in the Dunn Lewis Centre. The funeral home organised to live stream the funeral for friends and family that couldn't make it on the day. The Ulladulla High School also organised with the funeral home to live stream the funeral in the school hall.

Picking the main song for Zoie's funeral was easy. Zoie had picked her own funeral song. One day I had 'Angel' by Sarah McLachlan playing at home and Zoie and I had sung our little hearts out to it. As the song ended, Zoie said, 'That song is so sad. That is my funeral song'.

'Mine too', I said.

Simon asked for two more songs. He said I needed another sad one to play with a slide show of photos and a happy song to play at the end. A happy song, for fuck's sake. This was not a party I was planning. How am I supposed to find a happy song while planning my daughter's funeral? I was devastated. In a dark pit of misery. I didn't have an inch of happiness in me.

I got Zoie's laptop out and played her Spotify play list in the background. I sat on my verandah as all my friends and family came and went, listening for a song to pop out to me. Many of Zoie's songs were from the 80s and 90s genre. Many I also had in my own playlist. I could not find a happy, feel-good song. Even the 'happy' songs made me sad.

For two days, I had one song stuck in my head. 'Keep Your Head Up' by Andy Grammar. It was in both mine and Zoie's playlists. I thought it must be a sign; a message from Zoie to keep living life.

Finally, after 12 long days, Zoie's funeral was held on Monday, 13 July. We had over 220 people in attendance at the Dunn Lewis Centre, over 100 people at the high school hall and over 800 devices connected for the live stream.

There were blue paper cranes lining the stage at the front of the auditorium. Two large photo boards were on the stage, filled with a collage of photos of Zoie, and a photo of Zoie on a large projector screen hung front and centre from the ceiling above the stage. I was numb. I couldn't breathe properly, let alone speak. I sat frozen in my seat staring at Zoie's coffin and Zoie's photo in front of me. The funeral director, Simon, read out beautiful stories and memories of Zoie from myself, Zoie's father and one of her teachers. 'Angel' by Sarah McLachlan and 'Jealous of the Angels' by Donna Taggart played as we watched a slide show of photos.

I regret not getting up and speaking about my daughter myself. I would have liked a family member or one of Zoie's friends to say something, to make it a little more personal, but none of us felt capable of that. As 'Keep Your Head Up', by Andy Grammar played, Simon asked me at the end of the service, if the boys wanted to wheel Zoie's coffin out. I asked them, but without warning or preparation, they were put on the spot and said no. They were a mess and not thinking clearly either. Like me, they were just numb, frozen in their seats. This was not something I had even thought about beforehand, but thinking back on it now, it would have been nice if Zoie's brothers had wheeled her out.

I wanted a private wake at mums with our closest friends and family, and Zoie's close friends, but with Covid restrictions, we could only have 20 people in a house and my close family was more than that, so we had a small wake with tea, coffee and finger food at the Dunn Lewis Centre following the funeral. My close friends and family then went to the ExServos club.

Days later, we collected Zoie's ashes and urn from the funeral home. Aaron buckled her in the car, and we brought our girl home. Zoie now sits on her memorial mural buffet in our lounge room until we buy our own home and make a memorial garden for her there.

diary

Wed, 15/7/2020

Dear diary,
All the kids are at their other parents for a week. All our visitors have gone home. Local friends and family have returned to work. Their lives go on, but not ours. The house is so quiet. I think about Zoie every minute of every day. I miss Zoie talking to me at dinner. I miss her giggle. My girl will never finish school, get her first job, travel. I will never see my daughter have a boyfriend, get married or have babies. This is too soon. I didn't get enough time with her. She will miss out on so much of her life.

I had a rough, emotional day today. I just want to be with Zoie.

Fri, 17/7/2020

Dear diary,
My days are spent pacing up and down the house. I don't know what to do with myself. I don't want to see anyone or talk to anyone. Being with Aaron is the only time I feel calm. I can't sleep for more than a few hours at a time.

6

REMINDERS

After the funeral, all our extended family and friends went home. Our local friends and family stopped coming every day. The abundance of flowers slowly died, one bunch at a time, and were thrown in the bin.

The boys went to their other parents for a week and the house was quiet. Too quiet. It was good and much-needed time for Aaron and I to have alone, to grieve without the kids. Though we didn't know what to do with ourselves. We were not yet ready to leave the house. We didn't want to see or talk to anyone that was not close family. We would pace, mindlessly, up and down the house and watch movies. We took our two dogs for a walk most days, just to get out of the house and move, but were careful to avoid busy areas. We did our shopping online for a couple of weeks. Going to the shops meant the likely possibility of running into someone we knew, which sent our anxiety into overdrive.

The everyday, mundane things were hard to do. I would notice Zoie's clothes stopped coming through the washing. I would still subconsciously check the size on tags to tell the difference between Zoie and Charlie's school shirts, or some of my clothes that looked like Zoie's.

I would knock on Charlie's door to wake him up for school and then automatically go to Zoie's door. Oh, that's right. Zoie's not here.

It was torture cooking dinner without Zoie chatting away to me like she usually would. It was painfully quiet. I would stand numbly in the kitchen, blankly staring into Zoie's room like I was waiting for her to come out. I drowned out the pain with a few wines while I cooked, with tears streaming down my face.

I would get out seven plates to dish up for dinner when I only needed six. I couldn't stand the sight of Zoie's empty chair at our eight-seater dining table, so I shortened it down to a six-seater table by taking out the middle attachment. Her empty chair was just a painful reminder that she wasn't coming home. It was like being throat punched at every dinner.

I hated not having 'Zoie's' bedroom after I had cleared it out and moved Tyson into it. I felt like I had moved her out. I felt so guilty, like Zoie was going to come home from a long overseas holiday and want her room back. I missed having a pretty girl's room. I needed a space just for Zoie. I created a memorial mural in the lounge room and added a photo of Zoie's room, as it was.

Some people don't know if they should say anything to you about your loss. Maybe they just don't know what to say.

Some people don't want to remind you of your loss. Bringing up Zoie doesn't remind me. I don't forget that she died. It reminds me that you still care. It reminds me that others are still missing her too. In my opinion, it is better to say something than nothing at all. A simple 'I'm sorry' is fine. It lets me know you care and are there for me and leaves it up to me to open up to you or not.

Two weeks passed and the school holidays were over. The kids were going back to school. They were still traumatised, but they put on a brave face and tried to ignore their pain and grief, like a lot of men do. They wanted to go back. They were ready to socialise again. I guess being with their mates made it easier to push their troubled thoughts aside.

I wasn't ready. I had to drive again. I had to drive past that damn corner every day to get Charlie to school. Every time I'd drive past that corner, for months, I'd picture Zoie lying there, dead on the road. School zones were the worst. Doing the school pick-up and drop-off every day, for every bus I saw, I would picture Zoie hitting it and going underneath the bus. I would hold in my tears. Breathe, Karina. Just breathe. The kids will be at school soon and then you can let it all out. I dropped Charlie at the high school, now on the other side, so he didn't have to cross the road, and then I would drop the younger three boys at the primary school. As soon as the last child got out and closed the door, I would burst into tears.

Changes to the road around that corner began not even a week after the accident. The stop sign was moved forward a few meters. White line markings were added on St Vincent Street, clearly displaying a no driving or parking area. By the time school went back, there were water-filled barriers around the corner as a temporary fix, to be replaced with a fence not long after.

Ulladulla High School is on its own standalone block and only had one school crossing to the Ulladulla Public School on the north side. There is an entry and exit gate on every side of the high school, except for the north side where the crossing is. The main entry to the high school and the bus pick-up area is on South Street on the south side of the school, with another gate on both the east and west sides of the school. On the east side is St Vincent Street, the street of Zoie's accident. Other than the highway, St Vincent Street is the next main road to pass through town. Coles and Aldi both back onto St Vincent Street opposite the high school. It is a busy intersection with hundreds of children crossing along that whole east side of the school every morning and afternoon.

The Ulladulla area had a population of a little over 16,000 in 2019. The school is the only high school in our area and is overpopulated, with 1,198 students in 2018. It has become even busier since then. The high school takes in students from the surrounding two primary schools, which are also overpopulated.

There was no crossing. No traffic lights. Not even a median strip in the middle of the road. I was so angry. Where was the road safety for our kids? When Aaron and I saw the minimal road changes immediately after Zoie's accident, it pissed us off. To us, it was a clear sign from council and NSW roads and transport that they knew changes needed to be made and it took our daughter being killed there for them to act. Just some line markings and a fence were not good enough. We wanted traffic lights on the intersection of St Vincent and South Streets and a school pedestrian crossing on the east (St Vincent Street) and west (Camden Street) sides of the school.

There were many complaints and requests made to council and NSW roads and transport by me and the wider community for a school pedestrian crossing and traffic lights. Finally, in June 2021, almost one year after Zoie's death, work started on a pedestrian crossing on St Vincent Street.

Tues, 21/7/2020

Dear diary,

Met with our lawyer to start a claim against the bus company's CTP insurance. Thank God for Noel stepping in to be our middleman. I was completely lost and didn't know the first place to start. My mind is a mess and there is way too much information for me to process. We were told that the insurance will pay for the funeral, our medical bills and loss of wages, but there is no compensation payout because it goes off my psychological injuries from the accident, not Zoie's loss of life. Like losing your daughter's life because of someone running a stop sign is not relevant. If Zoie had lived, but was disabled for life, then we would be compensated, but because I am not injured, I'm not entitled to compensation. I am so pissed off. Like yeah, we'll pay your wages till you get back on your feet. You are sad now, but you'll get better.

~

The kids are back at school now. Charlie won't go near that corner or even look at it. I have to drop him on the other side of the school now and he won't walk home, not that we would let him now anyway, so we pick him up each afternoon. Driving past that corner every day, and any school zone now, is torture. Every bus I see, I picture Zoie going under it. I burst into tears as soon as I have dropped the younger three boys at school. I have a knot in my stomach and my chest is heavy like it is being crushed. I can't breathe. I feel like I'm drowning.

Wed, 22/7/2020

Dear diary,

Zoie has been gone for three weeks today. Aaron and I are nervous and anxious about driving now, especially at intersections and when we see pedestrians. I have a constant knot in my upper stomach. I am not numb anymore. I can feel every bit of my heartache. I can't bear the thought of *never seeing Zoie again. I feel so empty and depressed. I don't look forward to anything anymore. I don't see the beauty in life, the sun, the ocean. I am only just holding back tears all day, every day.*

I'm okay for a short while when I'm busy and push all thought of Zoie and her accident to the back of my mind. I just can't think about it or talk about it for long before the tears are back.

Only getting a few hours broken sleep each night. I wake up exhausted.

7

NOT COPING

Your child is not supposed to die before you. I have always been a strong person. I have experienced sexual abuse, emotional domestic abuse, had a miscarriage, skin cancer and breast cancer, but losing my one and only daughter was too much. After the funeral, the shock and numbness were gone. I was just left with the pain.

I hated being in public for fear of not being able to hold my composure. I felt like everyone would see me and know who I was and be like, 'Oh, look, that is that girl's mum'. Or I would fear people judging me like I shouldn't be out. That I should be a crying mess, not able to get out of bed.

Every song now means something different. All the lyrics describe Zoie or my pain. Even a love song would remind me that Zoie will never have her first love, marriage, or kids.

Seeing other blonde-haired girls would be a trigger for me. I would pause and stare because, for a moment, they would look like Zoie. All my nieces are blonde. I would watch them laughing and doing cartwheels on the beach and it would bring me to tears. Zoie loved doing cartwheels.

One day, I was sitting in the waiting room at the dentist. Charlie and Riley were getting braces. There was a woman and her teenage daughter sitting next to me laughing together at something on their phone. They appeared to have a close bond, just like Zoie and I. I felt the wave of pain coming on again. Pressure crushing my chest, a lump in my throat, the tears building. I had to run to the bathroom and burst into tears. I let myself cry for a few moments, then splashed my face and returned to the waiting room, just like nothing had happened.

I didn't want to go on without Zoie. I once loved life. I saw the beauty in everything around me; the sun, the moon, the ocean, plants. Now I was living in a dark world. I could not find the beauty in nature anymore. I didn't enjoy socialising. Sometimes I would let out a forced smile or even catch myself laughing and I would think to myself, 'What are you smiling about? You're not happy, you liar. You are being fake'.

I had some sleeping pills given to me by some well-meaning family and friends. They knew I wasn't sleeping at night. I had constant thoughts about taking them all at once. I wanted to sleep and never wake up. I wanted to be with Zoie. I saved the pills in my bedside drawer.

I would spot a big tree while driving up the highway and imagine putting my foot down and running straight into it. I would see the big, flat grill on the front of an oncoming truck and imagine driving head on into it. Suicide was never my plan or intention. I don't think I could ever carry it out, but it signified the depth of my longing to be with Zoie. I just wanted to see her again and death was the only way that was going to be possible.

I would then feel guilty for feeling like this. I have an amazing family. The best husband. My boys. My boys still needed their mum. They were hurting too. I had to be there for them. I had to be strong for them. Show them that they can go on. I was so scared that they would feel the way I did, and I couldn't stand the thought of losing another child.

After about five months, I hit rock bottom. I hated life. I was miserable, but I wanted to be strong for my family. I went to my doctor and told her that I really wasn't coping. I was finally prescribed an antidepressant. I was reluctant to take it. I didn't want to depend on medication. I didn't want to be drowsy but, all I could think about was missing Zoie and wanting to be with her. I thought that if I just took all my sleeping pills, I'd be with Zoie. 'No. No. I can't do that.' I had seen what suicide did to a close friend and her remaining family members, and the pain they live with every day. The ripple effect of more suicides. No. I couldn't do that to my parents, Aaron, or our boys.

Five months after Zoie's death and after much hesitation, I started taking the antidepressants. I'm now glad that I did. They helped me to keep going.

Within three weeks, I was calmer. I couldn't see the light at the end of the tunnel, but there was hope that one day I would.

I had so many thoughts going through my head that I had to get out. I found writing so cathartic, so I wrote in my diary every night from day one and, soon after, I started writing this book.

It would all get too much for me at times. I had to switch off and think about something else. Anything else. For the first six months, I read many books. I watched many Netflix series. I made a memorial mural and several photo collages. I also went to the gym several times a week. A year on, I started some home decor renovations and was back at work. This all helped to pass the time but didn't ease my pain. I was over the gym. Over work. I felt like I wanted to go on a soul-searching holiday or move out of town. I wanted to run away and escape my reality. I just wanted to feel complete happiness again, but what I needed was impossible. I needed Zoie back.

8

COUNSELLING AND MEDIUMS

We found it really hard to find counselling in our small town. Everyone was fully booked after the Currowan fires and now from Zoie's accident. About two months after Zoie's accident, I found a psychologist.

I saw her regularly for the first six months. I don't know why I kept going back. I don't think she helped me. Maybe I should have tried to find someone else but, at the time, I didn't believe that anyone or anything could help me. Nothing was going to bring Zoie back and that's all I wanted. The counselling sessions just got me to talk about how I was feeling and what I did to cope. I saw no point in continuing my sessions. I spoke openly with friends and family and that's all I was doing there as well. My psychologist would tell me I was doing all the right things and I was doing great, but she offered nothing that helped ease my pain.

I tried organising the boys to see a counsellor but, due to the lack of availability in our area and Covid, these had to be phone consultations. Boys don't open up at the best of times and now they were expected to open up to a stranger over the phone. Like me, they saw no point. The boys wouldn't open up to a counsellor, so it was pointless sending them. You can only get out what you put into counselling.

I looked deeper into meditation. I read a lot about psychic mediums and the spiritual world. I knew Zoie's spirit was still here with me. I could feel her. I just couldn't talk to or hear her.

I would often think about what heaven is like. Is it beautiful, full of love and happiness? What does Zoie do there? Is she having fun? Is she with our past loved ones? Where is she?

That is when I came across Charmaine Wilson. She is a psychic medium in Australia who won the TV show, 'The One', a few years back. I love how Charmaine is so down-to-earth and will tell it how it is. She is not an airy-fairy hippy that will tell you basic information that could relate to anyone. She is always specific and accurate in her readings. She has had a rough life, and also lost her daughter in a car accident and many other loved ones, so she is very familiar with grief.

Charmaine and her books are the main thing that got me though my grief. I started to make sense of Zoie's death and my grief. Charmaine helped me to understand the spirit world and that made me feel closer to Zoie. I highly recommend Charmaine Wilson's books, The Healing Art of Spirit and Spirit Children, to any newly bereaved parent. Charmaine helped me more than any counsellor.

Aaron was my rock. He always has been. He was the only one I would feel comfortable trying to explain how I was really feeling to, because he got it. He felt it too. Aaron would try to be strong for me, but he was broken too. He was so angry. Angry at the bus driver. Angry at the lack of road safety. He would go into the garage away from me and the kids and punch the old spare-drinks fridge. I would know what he was doing and follow him in there. As soon as he saw me, he would stop immediately and just look at me with his hands up, as if in surrender. We would just stand there crying and holding each other. It broke me to see my strong man so broken. He just wanted to be strong for me. To hide his pain. It was like we would take it in turns to have our ups and downs and hold each other up. Aaron hated that he was the one to break the news to me, all his family and work colleagues. 'It was our girl', was all he was able to say, and they knew what he was talking about. Being a small town, everyone new about the accident almost immediately.

Sat, 12/9/2020

Dear diary,

Aaron is back at work now and I need to keep busy. I go to the gym and do a class a few mornings a week. It actually has been helpful to clear my mind. On gym days, I can hold back the tears a little easier. Not yoga though. I lay on the floor in yoga, quiet and breathing at the beginning and end of the class. My mind is too quiet, and it leaves room for memories of Zoie to seep in. I lie there crying every time.

~

I see a psychiatrist almost weekly. I don't know why I keep going back. I don't think she is helping at all. She just gets me to talk about what I'm doing and thinking. I do that with my family anyway. Talking about it doesn't help. She says I'm doing everything right. She says that I'm doing well. What would she know? She has never lost a child. She has just read textbooks to tell her what to say to me. I don't feel like I'm doing very well at all. Talking doesn't make the pain go away. I don't think anything will help. I don't see an end to this shitty life I now live. This is just my life now. Missing my daughter, hating life and pretending that I'm okay.

Mon, 26/10/2020

Dear diary,

For the last two months, Aaron has been back at work. The kids are back at school. Maybe I should go back to work. I'm okay while I'm busy and I'll be busy at work. I called my boss and I'm back on the roster in two weeks. Oh shit, am I ready for work? What if I break down? I can't even hold a conversation. I'm an air head and can't think properly. How am I going to work? Its only two days a week and I won't do medications until I am comfortable. I work with some lovely people. They'll have my back. I can do this.

Sun, 1/11/2020

Dear diary,

Zoie, where are you? Where is heaven? What does heaven look like? Is it beautiful and peaceful? How do you spend your days? Are you happy?

I miss my girl so much. I have a pack of sleeping pills in my bedside table. Maybe I could take those, all at once. Then I could be with my baby girl. I would be happy and free from this hell. No, I couldn't hurt Aaron and the boys like that. My boys need their mum to get them through their pain of losing their sister. I couldn't put my mum through the pain I feel now. I guess I just have to suck it up and live in pain and misery.

~

I'm really anxious about going back to work. I think it is too soon and I'm just wanting to be okay. Fake it till I make it, I guess.

I cry more often than not. I'm exhausted all the time. I still don't sleep well at night, strangely, after Aaron goes to work. It's like I am calm and relaxed when Aaron is with me.

I think my cat, Baily, can sense how I'm feeling. She has been my shadow. She follows me everywhere. She jumps up to sit on me as soon as I sit down. She reaches up and taps me on the leg when I am in the kitchen making a cuppa. She sleeps right next to me in bed. When I kick her off the bed, she jumps right back up. If I lock her out of the room, she scratches at the door. She is like my support animal.

9

GRIEF

The way I describe grief is that it's like you are a rock island in the middle of the ocean. You are stuck. Still. Numb. Frozen. You can't move. Can't speak. All your emotions are the ocean around you. There are so many emotions. Sometimes all at once and, even though you are a rock, you are still human and can feel the blunt force of all of them. Sometimes they are just a gentle ebb and flow. At other times, they are huge waves crashing over you, completely submerging you under water. Your chest feels like it is being crushed and you can't breathe. Then suddenly, the water recedes and you can take that lifesaving gulp of air. These waves happen several times a day for a few months. Although they never go away for good, they do gradually happen less often.

Somewhere around two-to-four months after Zoie's death, I began to feel strangely calm. I thought that maybe I was getting better. Man was I fooled. Apparently, this is a normal thing for bereaved parents. This is the eye of the storm. I actually got much worse before I got better. The ocean began to stir yet again, getting rougher and stronger. I was being dragged back down beneath the surface. My chest felt like it was being crushed. I couldn't breathe. Grief runs through my veins like a burning poison. Then, for what feels like an eternity, I release it all out in one breath like John Coffee in the movie, 'The Green Mile'. I was left winded, defeated and empty.

I feel like there is a pane of glass, like a one-way mirror, between us and heaven. Zoie can see and hear everything I do, but I can't see or hear her; yet I can feel that she is close. Just in front of me. I just want to punch the glass and break the barrier between us, but it is invisible and can't be penetrated. Zoie is so close, yet so far. It is frustrating.

After about six months, I was not numb anymore. I still felt the ebb and flow, or the huge crashing waves, only now I also got thrown around with them. This was sink or swim time. I needed to become strong in the mind. Find a hobby. Meditate. Exercise. Write in a diary or poetry. Anything to keep me calm and clear my head. I don't know if I was trying to keep my head above water, or if I just learned to hold my breath until the water receded again.

For me, I found meditation, the gym, antidepressants and writing in my diary daily, helped.

Meditation helped to clear my mind. To quiet all the thoughts in my head, especially at night. I would practice just focusing on my breath. It was a constant battle in my mind each night. I would take a deep breath in, filling my mind, body and soul with clean, positive energy and then, with that newfound energy, I could ball up the dark, depressed, negative energy I called the Demon and release it from my body with a long exhale.

I had never been much of a gym person before. I still don't really like the gym equipment, but I do enjoy the group classes, especially boxing. Doing exercise was great for me to release all my negative energy. I needed to move; walk, run, box, swim, anything to get the blood flowing. If I didn't exercise, all that grief, all that negative energy just sat inside my body, like a poison. I would then feel like I was stuck in thick mud up to my neck.

After much hesitation, I took an antidepressant. After two weeks, I was starting to feel a little better. I had more patience with my boys. I cried less often. I enjoyed making new memories with the family. Life was not fun or easy, but it was bearable again.

Over time, maybe six to twelve months, my grief was less intense. It will never really go away for good because grief is love with nowhere to go. It is all that love you want to give but cannot. All that unspent love builds up. It builds up in the corner of your eyes, the lump in your throat and in the hollow part of your chest. For a bereaved parent, that love doesn't die when their child dies; it just gets built up stronger and stronger, and we can't give any of that love to that child. We can't talk to them or ask them how their day was. Kiss them. Cuddle them. Buy things for them. Celebrate with them.

I don't just mourn the loss of my daughter; I mourn the loss of the future I would have had with Zoie. I now will never see Zoie graduate from school. Zoie will never have her first boyfriend and heart break. I will forever think about what Zoie would look like now. Zoie will never get her first job. I will never see her get married. I will never see Zoie have children. I will now never have a mother-daughter relationship again.

There are many stages of grief, but the main five stages of grief are: denial and shock, anger, bargaining and guilt, depression and acceptance. I went through all these several times over. Sometimes all at once.

Denial and Shock

Denial hit me instantly, as soon as I was told about Zoie's death. I just couldn't understand that Zoie had died on that same corner where she had crossed every day. I hadn't identified her body, so how could they be sure it was Zoie? I knew the truth, deep down, but my brain just couldn't process it. I would keep waiting for her to walk through the door. I often imagined Zoie was away on holiday somewhere, and that she would be back one day.

Anger

I had never been an angry person before Zoie, but now I was. I was angry with everyone. I was angry at the bus driver. I was angry with anyone that had a different opinion to mine about Zoie's accident. I was angry at Zoie for leaving me and putting me through all this pain, and I was angry at myself for feeling this way.

I was angry at the bus driver for a long time. I knew he had not stopped at the stop sign. It was his job to get children home safely! He drove around that same corner every day. He would have known how busy it was and should have known to be extra vigilant for children crossing the road. I was even angrier when he pleaded not guilty in court. What a coward, I thought. I just wanted to see a little remorse from him for what he had done.

I was angry at people in the community gossiping about my daughter's accident. It really pissed me off when I heard people saying that the bus driver had done nothing wrong and that it was Zoie's fault.

I was angry with Zoie. I came to believe that we all, as souls, choose our life, how we live and when and how we die. I was angry at Zoie for wanting to live such a short life and hurting me like this. I was angry with myself for being angry at Zoie. My every thought and every word was about Zoie, or my grief, and it started to piss me off.

Bargaining or Guilt

I would often have all the 'what if' questions running through my mind. They would drive me insane. What if the driver had stopped? What if there was a crossing at the school? What if there were traffic lights? Would this still have happened? If only I had picked Zoie up that day. If only Covid still had the schools closed, Zoie would have been safe at home. Didn't I teach her to cross the road properly? I made every promise under the sun to bring my girl back. I felt guilty for not enjoying life when I still had an amazing husband and four beautiful boys. I felt guilty that I couldn't keep my baby safe. It's my job as a parent to protect my children. I felt guilty for being so depressed and emotionally unavailable to my husband and the boys.

Depression

I got to know depression well. We were not friends. I called my depression the Demon. It sucked every little bit of joy and happiness out of me. I knew I still had an amazing, supportive family. I still loved them with every inch of my being, but I couldn't enjoy them. I couldn't play and have fun with my boys. I didn't enjoy socialising with friends. It just wasn't fun, and I'd prefer to be at home. It wasn't until I finally gave in and took an antidepressant that I began to see glimpses of the old me, to see beauty in the world and enjoy life again.

Acceptance

For me, acceptance is not a final stage of grief where I am better or happy again. It doesn't mean that I have moved on or gotten over the loss of Zoie. It means that I have accepted that my time with Zoie is now over.

My first step towards acceptance and feeling better was to decide that I was not going to stay in this pain and misery anymore. I had the rest of my life to live, whether I liked it or not, and I didn't want to spend it being sad and angry and depressed. I had to allow myself to grieve and hurt, when needed, but also allow myself to live and love life again and know that this is okay.

I now feel fortunate and so thankful that I had Zoie in my life for 14 years. Zoie was a blessing. A gift that I had to give back much sooner than I was ready for. I have accepted that Zoie is gone, but I have not and don't think I ever really will accept the way she died. The only way I could come to terms with Zoie's death was to believe something Charmaine Wilson said: We are all souls living a human experience, so that we can learn lessons and grow. Our home is heaven or the spirit world. Before becoming human, we, as souls, choose the life we want to live, and the time and way we die, before going back home to heaven.

It took me a while to get to this point. Why would Zoie choose to put us through so much pain? Why would she choose to die in such a tragic way? Why would Zoie want to live such a short life?

I believe that Zoie's soul just didn't like living a long human life. I don't blame her either. With all the evil in the world, Aaron and I have always said that hell is here on Earth.

I have accepted Zoie's death, but that is not to say that I don't still have my bad days. I still miss Zoie immensely. I still cry daily because it is just so unbearably hard and painful to live without my daughter. I am jealous of Zoie and think it is unfair that I have to wait so long without her for my turn to return home to heaven.

~

With grief, after losing a child, comes stress and posttraumatic stress disorder (PTSD). Stress can cause many symptoms, including shaking, skin break outs, irritable bowel syndrome (IBS), pain, nausea, headaches, sleeplessness and fatigue. With PTSD, you can also experience flashbacks, nightmares, intrusive thoughts, avoiding reminders and anxiety, or looking out for danger.

In the early days, as soon as I shut my eyes, I would get images of the bus hitting Zoie and her body going under the wheel. Or I'd see Zoie lying dead on the road when I drove past that corner every morning for school drop-off.

I would have nightmares that left me tired and scared to go to sleep. Because I was tired from my constant thoughts, I often had a headache. I got more pimples than I had since I was a teenager and I often had diarrhea.

Every time I see a police car, I remember pulling up to my house and seeing a police car parked out the front and two officers standing with Aaron on the lawn, and my feeling hopeless and broken as my body began to shake.

Every time I hear a siren, I am thrown back to the time of the accident, hearing all the sirens for hours, as I searched all over town for Zoie and sat at home in utter shock and heartache after being told my baby girl had died.

Eventually, this got too much. Every day that I drove past that damn corner, I practiced changing the image in my mind of Zoie dead on the road, to an image of Zoie standing there, smiling and waving at me. On some days this worked and on others it didn't, but it did get easier over time.

diary

Mon, 23/11/2020

Dear diary,

I have been feeling really shit. I am really depressed. I have not been able to hold back tears all day, every day. I have a short temper and snap at the kids. I don't enjoy life or appreciate Earth's beauty like I used to.

I often think about Zoie in heaven, what she does there, who she's with, where it is and wonder what it looks like?

I think about suicide, not to the point of wanting to do it or that I actually would, but as being the only way that I would be able to be with Zoie again.

I think heaven would be beautiful and peaceful and that hell is here on Earth. What keeps me here is my family. Aaron, the boys, my parents and siblings. I could never put them through that much pain and grief. I don't want them to feel the pain I feel now. I spoke to the doctor and got a script for an antidepressant.

I had to stop work again. I need to focus on me and my family.

Tues, 24/11/2020

Dear diary,

The kids have been shitty and playing up. They are really struggling and it tears me up knowing that I can't take their pain away.

I feel a pain in my chest like it is being ripped down the middle. I picture Zoie dead on the road every time I drive past that bloody corner and see Zoie going under every passing bus I see on school pickup and drop-off. I burst into tears as soon as the kids are out of the car, suck it up while I go into the gym and then cry for the rest of the day.

Sat, 28/11/2020

Dear diary,

Today was the first day since Zoie died (five months ago) that I didn't cry once all day until I went to bed. I think the antidepressants are starting to work. I also feel guilty for feeling okay. I know I shouldn't, but I do.

10

HOW TO HELP A BEREAVED PARENT

I hated hearing the words, 'It will get easier with time'. I didn't like hearing that 'I was strong, inspirational and doing well', because I didn't believe it. I felt like I was falling apart and not giving 100% to my family. For a while, I didn't want to be strong. I didn't want to be okay because I would then feel guilty for being okay. Like I was moving on too fast. I felt like Zoie would be looking down on me and seeing me to appear to be okay. I would beg, plead and apologise to Zoie. I'm so, so sorry, Zoie. Please forgive me. I'm not okay. I'm just pretending. I miss you so much that it physically hurts.

And I did pretend to be okay after a while because I simply got sick of being so miserable. Zoie was on my mind all day, every day. Zoie and my grief were all I would talk about, and it got annoying. After about six months, I got sick of always only talking about Zoie and my grief, so surely everyone else was sick of hearing about it too. So, I pretended to be okay. I tried to force myself to not talk about Zoie. My pain and excruciating longing to be with Zoie never went away or got better with time; I just learned how to live with it and ignore the pain.

I just wanted people to accept the fact that my loss could not be fixed. Don't tell me that time will heal all wounds. It doesn't! Don't tell me that Zoie is in a better place. I already know this and want to be in that better place with her! We have all said it at some point: 'Just let me know if there is anything I can do'. My advice is, don't ask a newly bereaved parent if there is anything they need or ask how you can help. In the first few weeks, I was in shock and had no idea what would help or what needed to be done. If they are anything like me, they probably won't want to bother you either. If you really want to help a grieving friend or family member, you can do things to make their day-to-day life easier.

Some examples that helped me in the first few weeks are:

- Make some meals that are easy to freeze and heat up.
- Do their washing, dishes, vacuuming.
- Do their shopping.
- Offer to babysit or have their surviving child over for a playdate with your child, if they are friends.
- Just sit with them, talk, or just listen.

People never know what to say to a bereaved parent. I think it is better to say something than nothing at all. Just a quick, 'I'm sorry for your loss', to acknowledge it, and then move on to what's going on in your own life. If you are wondering what else you can say, other than 'I'm sorry for your loss', here are some examples:

- You are in my thoughts and I'm here for you.
- Sending you my deepest condolences for the loss of Zoie.
- Sending all my love.
- My thoughts are with you and your family.
- I know you are hurting, but you are not alone. I'm here.

Often, when we know someone is grieving, our discomfort and not knowing what to say or do, keeps us from approaching the subject. There is no right or wrong thing to say. You don't even have to say anything. Just be there! Watch a movie together! Don't feel like you shouldn't talk about the person that died, like it will remind you of your loss. Zoie is on my mind all day, every day. You can't remind me that she is gone. I will never forget. Don't be afraid to talk about Zoie. If you see something that reminds you of Zoie, tell me. If I speak about Zoie or relive memories, relive them with me. If you didn't know Zoie well, don't be afraid to ask me about her. One of my greatest joys is talking about my daughter. For the first couple of weeks before Zoie's funeral, I loved having all my friends and family around me at home, just chatting about their days and making jokes, talking about 'the good old days'. It was comforting just having them there.

On the day that Zoie died, my friends, Rachele and Shelly, asked me if I wanted to start a 'go fund me' page so that Aaron and I could take time off work and not worry about our finances. We immediately said no. We have never been people to ask for help or handouts. We were already overwhelmed by all the flowers, cards and food sent to us, so we were not going to ask anyone for money. This was our problem and we would figure it out. Somehow.

The next day, Rachele and Shelly were asked by people in the community if there was a fundraiser for us and told that someone wanted to start a 'go fund me' for Aaron and I. Rachele eventually convinced me that the community wanted to help and was going to start a fundraiser for us, whether or not we wanted it. I agreed for the girls to set one up and was completely stunned and overwhelmed when it reached over $4,000 in half an hour.

In hindsight, Aaron and I are extremely thankful now that we did agree. We are eternally grateful to all those who donated, as it allowed us to take as much time off work as we needed. We could just be with our boys and grieve and not have the extra stress of worrying about how we were going to pay all our bills. We were able to pay off all our debts completely. Our wages were covered by the bus company's CTP insurance until we each returned to work.

One thing I didn't know to do was to apply for compensation. Because Zoie died from a motor vehicle accident, we were entitled to compensation through the bus company's CTP insurance. I had not thought of compensation until I spoke to the forensic pathologist, who told me to look up SIRA for compensation. I had never heard of SIRA. I had no idea how it all worked. I was so overwhelmed and still numb, so I asked Noel, my stepfather, to look into it for me.

All motor vehicles have registration and compulsory third party insurance (CTP). The CTP is paid to cover the cost of any injuries, damages and death in the event of an accident. You need to know the CTP insurer of the vehicle at fault, then hire a (no win no pay) lawyer to claim compensation through the CTP insurance.

We were able to claim personal injury (psychological) compensation, which paid a percentage of our loss of wages while we were not working, the funeral costs and medical expenses, including counselling.

After two years, we may be able to apply for common law damages, which is a lump-sum compensation payment because we were diagnosed with PTSD. It is classed as 'more than a minor injury'.

I suffer from and have been diagnosed with PTSD following Zoie's death, as I believe every bereaved parent would. When Zoie died, my whole world crumbled to pieces, never to be the same again. I changed in many negative ways. I felt robbed of my future with Zoie. I had horrific visions and thoughts. I had loss of sleep. I will never get my daughter back. When it comes to compensation, I am expected to get over it eventually and move on with life. There is no lump-sum compensation payment for Zoie's death, only for our psychological injuries. It only covers income wages and medical expenses while I'm not able to work, so, if Zoie were an adult with a job that supported her own family, or Zoie had survived, but was disabled for life and in any way not able to work, then she would be able to claim a compensation payment. But Zoie's death was not recognised as an injury that I suffered.

11

SUPPORTING THE KIDS WHILE GRIEVING

Surviving children can be the forgotten mourners after the death of a child. Often bereaved parents put the child that died up on a pedestal. They make their whole life about the child that died, which leaves the surviving children feeling not as important, like they will never be good enough. I was not going to let our boys feel that way.

We still had four boys and they were grieving the loss of their sister. They still needed their parents. They still needed love, attention and support. So, although all I wanted to do was lie in bed or sit on my verandah, I took the boys to the park, out for lunch and went to the movies.

One of Tyson's favorite memories with Zoie was making pancakes for breakfast on the weekends, so he likes to continue that tradition. Sometimes the boys would watch movies that Zoie liked.

It was impossibly hard for me to grieve and still be a good mum and wife at the same time. It was exhausting and, at times, I just wanted to lie on the lounge all day, every day, watching movies or reading. I wanted to escape my reality. I had already lost a child and my next biggest fear was to lose another child or my husband. I was terrified that my boys would be in so much grief that they might think about suicide. It was this fear that made me want to be there for them, to help them in any way that I could. I was equally terrified that if I withdrew too much and if I weren't the same wife, that Aaron would eventually have enough and leave. So, I made time for myself each day to just grieve. To feel my pain or to retreat and read. That way, I was able to give my time and energy to Aaron and the boys. I still made time to take the kids to the movies. I still made date nights or the odd weekend away with Aaron. We did a lot of family things together. Ironically, it was Aaron and the boys needing me to be a wife and a mum that kept me going. Without them, I probably wouldn't be here today.

Charlie was struggling with being back at that school. He was in the same year as Zoie and they shared some of the same friends. His anxiety would go into overdrive in class, but he didn't feel like he was able to leave the classroom without getting into trouble or being a nuisance. Maybe he just wanted to push on and be strong. I spoke to the principal, who then gave Charlie a leave pass to use whenever he needed to and arranged for him to speak with the school's emotional support person. I think that helped him relax. Maybe he just needed to be reassured that his feelings were valid.

I got a call from Tyson's school one day to come and pick him up. His teacher noticed that Tyson was teary at school and just holding it together. As soon as Tyson saw me when I got to the school office, he burst into tears and walked into my open arms. I asked him what happened. He replied, 'I just couldn't breathe'. It broke my heart to see my boys hurting so much and I couldn't fix it. Aaron and I often reminded the boys that if they were ever having a bad day at school, to just call one of us or go to the school office so they could call us to come and get them. We didn't want the boys feeling like they were trapped at school if grief suddenly snuck up on them, as it often does.

Aaron and the boys would like to ignore their pain and just get on with life. They would keep busy with work, school and social arrangements so that they didn't get a chance to think too much. The problem with this was that the negative energy would eventually build up and become too much to handle. They would break down in tears, become angry and frustrated or punch a brick wall. I told Aaron to hang the boxing bag up for him and the boys to hit. It worked well too. Aaron and the boys each would hit the bag every day. Sometimes for half an hour or sometimes just once as they passed by it. Either way, they were getting their negative energy out of their systems long enough to keep going.

Me, on the other hand, didn't ignore my grief. I allowed myself to feel it. I would make time for myself to write down what I was feeling, use my anger in the fight class at the gym or sing along to a sad song at the top of my lungs that expressed exactly how I was feeling. I would talk openly to anyone that wanted to listen about how I was feeling. When I felt the tears build up, I would just let them keep falling. I would allow myself to cry until I got it out of my system. Sometimes you just need a good cry.

Often a couple will take it in turns to be the strong one. This was the case for Aaron and I. It seemed to just work out that when I was having a bad day, Aaron was not too bad and he was able to comfort me and vice versa. When Aaron was having a tough time, I was able to be there for him. As we always have been, we were good at noticing when the other was feeling down, even when we would say we are okay. We would encourage each other to talk about what was on our mind and to write or punch the punching bag to release the negative energy.

If you are not the strong one, thank your partner for holding you up, but then ask them if they are okay. It's important to ask them how they are feeling and to give them options that might interest them to get their grief out.

You might be broken, but one day it will be better, and you don't want to wake up from your grief and be alone. So, be kind to yourself. Take time to grieve, but don't forget your surviving children and partner are hurting too.

I feel so lucky to have such a strong relationship with Aaron. I feel calmer and stronger when I'm with him. I am more comfortable going to the shops or being in a social gathering when I have Aaron by my side. Aaron is a baker, so he leaves early for work. I don't sleep well after he leaves for work in the morning.

We take it in turns to be the strong one. We talk openly to one another about how we are feeling, what are our triggers are and what comforts us. Aaron has been my rock. My safe place. He catches me when I fall, but he can be vulnerable too. He can tell me when he is struggling and what triggers him. This was comforting to me because it told me how much Zoie meant to him, how much he missed her too. It validated my feelings and I knew I wasn't alone.

~

Kids need honest, simple information. Your child may need your help to understand death. It is best to explain what has happened as simply and truthfully as you can. When I told the boys, I simply said, 'there has been an accident. Zoie died'. It was all I could get out between sobs, but it was all they needed.

Using the words 'death' or 'died' can avoid confusion for young children. If you say that someone has 'passed away' or 'gone to sleep', your child might be confused or frightened. If a child is told that someone they loved has gone to sleep forever, they might get scared to fall asleep and never wake up.

Younger children may not know what death means, so you might need to describe it and make sure they understand. For example, saying 'your sister was in an accident. Her body stopped working. She stopped breathing, so she won't be coming home ever again'. Explain to them that death is just as natural as birth. Everyone dies one day and, although people usually die when they are old or extremely sick with a terminal disease, young people can die too. When our time is up, it is up.

If you have more than one child, you might talk with the children together or separately. Thinking about how old your children are, as well as their different temperaments, can help you work out what is best.

Like adults, children might get angry or frustrated over the smallest things. They might cry more easily than they used to. They might appear calm and quiet when their minds are actually overloaded with anxiety and questions. And they will ask you these questions. Some you will be able to answer, but if you can't, it is ok to say you do not know and that you can find out.

Here are some questions that my boys asked me:

How did Zoie die?
Your child might want to make sense of the death. They might want to know what caused the death, so try to answer the question honestly and straight to the point. In my case, I told the boys, particularly Tyson, being the youngest at 9, that Zoie was hit by a bus, her body stopped working and she died instantly.

Will you die? Will I die?
Your child might start to realise that the people they love could

die. It is a good idea to let your child know that death is natural and that most people die only when they're really old and very sick. Death is nothing to be afraid of. It is a natural part of life.

What happens when you die?

How you answer this question depends on your family's personal or spiritual beliefs. You could talk with your children about these beliefs. My boys asked me this question, so I asked them what they believed? I said that I believe our soul leaves our body and goes to heaven. I believe heaven is here on Earth amongst us, but in a parallel universe. Heaven is filled with everyone and everything we love. And I believe each soul has a free pass to look in on our living universe whenever they like, so they don't miss us.

I explained to my boys that Zoie's spirit, or her soul, is still alive. She is in heaven. She is free, happy and in a place of love. It is only her body that died. It is kind of like your body is an avatar or vehicle, and you are your soul controlling it from the inside.

When your body dies, your soul just leaves that avatar or body and goes home to heaven.

What do we do with Zoie's body?

We had Zoie's body cremated, so when I was asked this by the boys, I very simply stated that we burnt it. I explained the process of Zoie's body being placed in her coffin and this being placed in a big oven that will burn, and that we can keep the ashes and scatter her in our favourite place or put her in a special garden.

Some people might want to hide their own emotions from their kids to protect them. I don't hide my emotions or tears from my boys, because I believe it teaches them about loss and that it's okay to feel any and all emotions. I would simply explain to them that I was crying because I missed Zoie.

~

It is no secret that a marriage can struggle after the death of a child. Grief is so personal and effects everyone differently. One spouse may want to be open and connect, while the other may want to retreat, shut down or keep busy with work or hobbies. You may not have the strength or energy to comfort each other or understand the other's grief pattern.

Intimacy can decline after you lose a child. You have that child and their death on your mind 24/7 so, naturally, you are not going to be in the mood. But you need to find a way to clear your mind so you can be in the moment with your partner. Physical and emotional intimacy is important in a marriage. People have a need to feel loved and appreciated; and that provides a sense of security and confidence. Without intimacy, you can become disconnected from your partner. You need to be completely open and honest with your partner about your sex life and intimacy. I believe that patience, affection and open communication are the key to keeping a happy marriage after the death of a child.

Aaron and I have always had a fun, vibrant and spontaneous sex life. Even after years of marriage, we still would flirt with each other often. After Zoie died, so did our sex life. We didn't even realise for a month or more, but once we did, we spoke openly about it. Through talking about it, we realised that we were both feeling the same way. We were both still very much attracted to each other and missed our sex life, but we both constantly had Zoie and our grief on our minds and were emotionally exhausted. That one conversation made all the difference. From then on, it was like we were able to flick our Zoie switch on and off just long enough to make some time for intimacy.

12

SPECIAL OCCASIONS AND DATES

There will always be dates of the year that will trigger my emotions and send me straight back to the day it happened.

For the first year, I was debilitated by every Wednesday, the 1st of every month, Mother's Day, our birthdays (mine being only three days after Zoie died), Christmas, and family holidays and gatherings. Zoie loved special occasions and would always make a big deal about them. Zoie would be the one to decorate and organise the presents. The boys, not so much.

The first of every month is always hard. Especially in the first year. It is another painful day reminding me that it is another month without Zoie. My world had stopped on the 1st, yet the days, months and years keep passing by.

On my first Mother's Day without Zoie, I was a mess. I was feeling pretty good in the days leading up to it and hadn't thought much about it. I thought it would just be another Mother's Day and that I'd be fine. On the morning of Mother's Day, I was crying within minutes of waking up.

Zoie was my first born; the one that made me a mum for the first time. This was the first Mother's Day without one of my babies since becoming a mum. I was broken all over again. I was rostered on to work that day. There was no way I could go in. As hard as I tried, I just couldn't stop crying. Instead of the usual quick 'Happy Mother's Day' in passing, the boys all spoiled me with hugs and presents, which just made me cry more because it reminded me of the effort Zoie would have made. I felt so loved and adored. I felt so blessed to have an amazing family, but I also felt the soul-crushing absence of Zoie.

Christmas had always been my favourite time of year. It was a time for being with family. Now my family was incomplete. It felt wrong to celebrate and be merry without Zoie, but I do it in her honour because Zoie loved Christmas. Zoie had made it a tradition to watch Home Alone each Christmas Eve. I continue this tradition in her honour, but my heart is full of sorrow, and I miss Zoie with all my being.

The first Christmas after Zoie died, all the boys were with their other parents for Christmas Eve so, on Christmas morning, it was just Aaron and I. It was painfully quiet. I cried all morning. I had a shower, applied some make up to hide my red blotchy face and somehow managed to pull myself together before picking up the boys and going to mums for Christmas lunch and dinner. I placed a butterfly tea light candle in the middle of the table to acknowledge Zoie. The kids all excitedly played with their cousins, opened their presents and smashed open a piñata.

I felt like I was watching my own life from the outside. I was filled with love and joy, surrounded by all my loved ones, yet I still felt an emptiness in my stomach. I had a heavy chest. It felt so wrong to celebrate Christmas when my family wasn't complete. Zoie should be there, and it was painfully obvious that she wasn't.

As I sat around the table, having a drink and a laugh, suddenly, out of nowhere, a wave came crashing over me again. I couldn't breathe. Tears built up in my eyes. I walked into mum's room, sat on her bed and cried painful, breathless sobs. It took about 10 minutes to get it out of my system before I splashed my face and went back to join everyone else.

diary

Tues, 8/12/2020

Dear diary,
Jacob has been randomly vomiting in the middle of the night, once a week. He is otherwise fine and the doctor can't find any reason for it. I think it is his grief. That bloody demon, secretly and silently getting him and he doesn't even realise it.

I have been feeling much better since taking my antidepressants. I am still tired and lacking energy. I don't sleep well after Aaron leaves for work at 2.30am. I am even looking forward to Christmas. I am also anxious about it because I don't know how I'll be on the day, but I am expecting it to be hard.

Wed, 23/12/2020

Dear diary,
It's two days before Christmas and the police detective on Zoie's case has just informed us that the bus driver has been charged with negligent driving occasioning death and failing to stop at a stop sign.

Finally, some closure, but what a time to bring all this up, right before Christmas.

Mon, 28/12/2020

Dear diary,
I am really missing Zoie. I can't bear the thought of bringing in the new year without my girl. I still have my moments daily when I can't hold back the tears, usually when I look at her photos. I just think of all she will miss out on. Starting year 10 with Charlie, the blessing of the fleet ball, her first job.

It was a beautiful day yesterday; Aaron and I took the boys to the beach. We all had a swim. I got out of the water first and stood on the shore watching my family. My husband was playing rough with the boys, tackling them in the waves. I had tears in my eyes. I was sad, thinking that I'm the only girl in my family now. Where is my princess doing cartwheels in the sand? It's not fair. Why did she have to leave me?

Sun, 28/1/2021

Dear diary,
I have been getting more and more anxious. I don't know if it's because I have been thinking about trying to go back to work again, if it's the boys starting at that high school or Charlie starting year 10, Zoie's year. Maybe it's all of it. I have had loose bowels every day for a couple weeks. I think it's from the stress and anxiety. I have been feeling good since Christmas, so maybe I'm starting to crash again.

Wed, 3/2/2021

Dear diary,
I have been thinking lately that I will go back to work soon. Mabey next month. I had to go to the doctor to renew my Certificate of Capacity form for this month. My usual doctor is on maternity leave, so I had to see a new doctor. The thought of seeing a new doctor, talking about it all again to someone that doesn't know my story and explaining why I can't work to a stranger really got to me. I sat, feeling nervous in the waiting room. My hands started to sweat; I even dry reached. After the long and torturous appointment, I got back in the car where Aaron was waiting for me and explained it to him and broke down in tears. After that reaction, I thought that maybe everyone is right. Maybe it is too soon to go back to work. I'll put work on hold a little longer. After all, it is Zoie's birthday next month and the month after that is the court case.

Sat, 13/2/2021

Dear diary,
I think about Zoie all the time. I worry that my memories of Zoie are fading and becoming less vivid.
Today, I pulled out Zoie's laptop and started writing a book about losing Zoie and my grief. It took me two-and a-half hours to write one-and-a-half pages because I couldn't stop crying, so it might take me a while. I have never written anything other than diary entries, so I don't know if it will be any good or if I'll even publish it, but, if nothing else, it could be good therapy for me to get it all out.

13

ZOIE'S ROOM

Zoie was a typical teenager and spent a lot of time in her room. For the first week after Zoie died, I kept Zoie's bedroom door shut. It was a painful reminder that my princess wasn't home and never would be again. I then began to miss Zoie's room. I couldn't have Zoie, but everything else of Zoie was in that room. Zoie's room was her castle and her bed, with a large, dull pink upholstered bed head, was her thrown.

The bedside table was complete with a pink bedside lamp and a small glass vase with pink and white flowers. The white dressing table had an attached tall rectangular mirror and consisted of a white and purple jewellery box and perfumes. Zoie kept her laptop on her light brown study desk, which was complete with photos, candles, a cup of pens and a cork board with her school calendar and some drawings and quotes pinned to it.

Zoie's room was so warm and bright, with the sun beaming in through her large window, covered with a white lace curtain, all day. Zoie's room was infused with her musky perfume. I would feel close to Zoie in there. I would often mindlessly wander in there, sit on her bed and talk to her and cry.

After Zoie died, I felt she was still a part of her room somehow, like her spirit was attached to it or something. I had placed a couple of the teddies from the roadside memorial, and the box of letters from the school students, on Zoie's bed. It was Zoie's room. Zoie's own space. I wanted to keep it as it was, as Zoie's room forever, but we were only renting and had plans to buy our own house soon, so we would have to clear it out one day anyway.

Charlie and Riley have their own room, but Jacob and Tyson have shared a room since they were babies. Jacob and Tyson had been fighting more often. Jacob would be a teenager soon and will want his own space. Zoie's room was not being used and, although Aaron and I were not ready, it was logical to move Tyson into Zoie's room.

On 6 March, it had only been eight months since Zoie died.

Aaron and I cleared out Zoie's room together and moved

Tyson in. We sorted through her things one item at a time.

I read all Zoie's notebooks and diaries. I held all her teddies. I touched every piece of her jewellery. I sorted Zoie's things into four piles: keep, throw, cousin, and sisters.

I wanted to keep everything but had no logical reason to. I was not going to just throw it all out or give Zoie's things away to a stranger. I needed to keep it all, if not for myself, then at least keep it in the family. That bedroom was Zoie's pride and joy and so was her family. So, that's what we did. We kept it in the family. We gave Zoie's bed and clothes to her cousin and a few toys, jewellery, and Knick knacks to Zoie's two (step and half) sisters.

I boxed up and kept a couple of Zoie's favorite hoodies, clothes and personal items. I keep her cushions on my bed. I placed the teddies from the roadside memorial on Zoie's memorial shrine at home. To that shrine, I added a photo frame containing six photos of Zoie's room, one with her lying on her bed that I had taken five months before she died.

I hate not having Zoie's room anymore. I feel like I have moved her out, when all I want to do is hold onto her. I wanted to keep her room just as it was.

I need space just for Zoie. I kept the teddies from her bed, the photos and a few knick knacks that made it 'Zoie's room'. I placed them on my shrine that I have for Zoie in our lounge room.

14

ZOIE'S BIRTHDAY

Zoie was my eldest child. My first born. The one that made me a first-time mummy. Our family tradition has always been that our children can choose what we have for dinner on their birthday. Zoie would usually choose Chinese or Indian. We didn't have a birthday party every year for the kids but, in her last few years, Zoie had a few of her friends over. I had never had one of my children's birthdays without them or not been able to say happy birthday.

Wednesday, 24 March 2021 was Zoie's 15th birthday. It was the first birthday we had to celebrate without her. The boys all felt good emotionally and went to school. I started the day with a good cry for an hour or so as I was inundated with many messages from family and friends sending me their love and thoughts. I also received a few messages from Zoie's friends with photos and videos of them and Zoie.

Once I got my cry out of my system, I freshened myself up, went into town for a few party decorations and picked up Zoie's chocolate mud cake that I had ordered a few days earlier. Then Aaron and I went out for a Chinese lunch, one of Zoie's favorites.

After we picked the boys up from school, we had a birthday party down by the water at the harbour. We decorated a table with a white tablecloth and stuck butterfly stickers all over it. I tied a pink 'Happy 15th Birthday' helium balloon to the table.

I thought Zoie's birthday was going to be terribly sad and tough, but it was actually the opposite. I wanted to celebrate Zoie's life, not her death, and that's what we did. It was a beautiful, magical day, filled with love and happiness. It was a hot, sunny, blue-sky day after a week of rain. We saw dolphins swimming out in the water.

We celebrated with all Zoie's loved ones, including her closest friends, all sharing our memories of Zoie. There were many hugs, smiles and laughter. After lighting a sparkler in the cake, we sang happy birthday to Zoie. We then released three butterflies. Butterflies symbolise transformation and hope for the afterlife. We watched them, one at a time, stretch and flap their wings before taking off into the air.

It would not be Zoie's party without food, so we had a cake, chips, party pies, quiche and sandwiches. We received several bunches of flowers, cards, and gifts. Our house once again resembled a florist in sight and smell.

For me, it was great to catch up with Zoie's friends. The girls were such a big part of Zoie's life and I felt I had lost them too when I lost Zoie. In a way, I feel connected to them through Zoie. I like to keep in touch with the girls, knowing Zoie would have had similar experiences to what the girls were. And I think the same is true for the girls. Maybe they feel connected to Zoie through me.

diary

Mon, 1/3/2021

Dear diary,

I have hit another low this week while sick with bronchitis. I'm still not sleeping well, and my emotions are always worse when I'm tired and run down.

Tyson drove me mad today with his constant talking and pointless questions. I have no patience at the moment. I don't want to cook dinner. I don't want to parent. I don't want to do anything.

I was dead tired last night, but still couldn't sleep. I eventually cried myself to sleep by about midnight.

Thurs, 11/3/2021

Dear diary,

I don't get the physical, crushing, drowning pain in the chest anymore. Now I just have a knot in my stomach. I am sad, depressed and miss Zoie more than I can put into words.

I see a new doctor now. She is great and makes me feel comfortable and listened to. She is thorough and pays extra attention to my mental health.

I feel like I have had something small stuck in my throat, like a tablet or grain of rice for months, and I have had trouble swallowing dry food. I also have a dry, constant cough. I think it might be asthma. All tests are clear, so I guess it's just stress.

Fri, 26/3/2021

Dear diary,

I am feeling strong, clear minded and have a longing to get my old self back again. I can talk and socialise with others again. I can hold a conversation and am happy to do so. I feel like I am ready to return to work gradually, but I'm not sure how I'll be after the court case, so I'll put it off until then.

Although I am feeling better and more like my old self, I still cry almost daily, as

I miss Zoie and think it is unbearably wrong, hard and fucked up to live without my daughter, and I often feel jealous of Zoie, like why do I have to wait so long for my turn to return home to heaven?

15

GOING BACK TO WORK

While I would watch medical shows on TV and do my online training modules for work, I realised that I liked my job. I was good at my job and I missed it. I had worked too long and hard to throw it all away, and I still wanted to further my career.

I attempted to go back to work twice in nine months. Each time I had many thoughts going through my mind. Can I go back? Do I want to go back? Is it too soon? Should I change jobs? Maybe I need a fresh start. Should I apply with the new aged care company being built in town?

The first time I went back to work was In November. I only lasted a week. It had only been four months. I was strangely calm. I was fine, as long as I was busy or had something to focus on. I thought, I am ok while I'm busy, so I can go to work. I'll be busy there. It will give me something else to think about and force me back into a normal routine again. Aaron had returned to work after two months. I felt guilty that Aaron was still struggling, being thrown around in the waves of grief and was back at work when I wasn't. Aaron was still hurting too and sucking it up. Maybe I should too.

I spoke to my boss and arranged to go back two weeks later. From that day on, I became increasingly anxious about returning to work. I felt guilty for trying to move on so soon. I was worried that it would be too much pressure on Aaron to work all morning, then do the school pick up and dinner while I was at work in the afternoon. I was worried that the boys still needed me home. Was it too much change all at once?

I returned to work in November for four days a fortnight. All my work colleagues gave me their condolences and seemed genuinely happy to see me back. Although I felt loved and supported by my colleagues and I was busy, I couldn't think about anything but Zoie. I felt lost, like I was new again. I couldn't think of what I was to do next. I couldn't time manage or prioritise. I was avoiding everyone as much as I could because I couldn't hold a conversation. I would walk the corridors at work with tears welling up in my eyes. Residents would buzz their call bell for assistance one after the other. I would wipe my eyes, take a deep breath and go to the resident. But my mind wasn't with the resident's needs. My mind was on Zoie and my pain. I was falling deeper and deeper into depression. I was missing Zoie. I just wanted to see her. To talk to her again. I wanted to be with Zoie, wherever that was.

On the third shift, I had a resident ask me to read out a passage from a card. It was a passage about loss and grief. I managed to read the whole thing. With tears in my eyes, I just couldn't hold it in. I left the room, sat in the hallway and cried. A work colleague came to comfort me, told me to go get a cuppa. 'No, I'll be ok', I said. I picked myself up and continued my shift.

I only did one more shift after that and stopped working again. I was not coping. It had only been four months after Zoie's death. It was way too soon and I couldn't focus. I was in a fog. I couldn't hold a conversation. I couldn't pretend to be okay anymore, and it wasn't safe or fair on my residents and colleagues when I wasn't able to focus or concentrate at work.

I hit rock bottom. I hated life. I felt no joy. I couldn't see the beauty in the simple things, like sunrises, sunsets, a full moon, dolphin's swimming, the sun glistening on the ocean, watching, and listening to the wild animals in the bush while camping, watching my children playing and laughing, swimming at the beach. These things used to fill my heart with joy. I used to find love, peace and pleasure in these simple things on Earth, but now it was all gone. All I felt now was pain, sadness and an excruciating longing to be with Zoie.

I told my doctor about how I was struggling and that I'd had to stop work again, so she put me on an antidepressant.

I had to go back to my doctor every month to renew my Certificate of Capacity form so that I could continue to receive my compensation payments while I was not working. In February, it had been seven months. The antidepressants seemed to be working. I thought I was doing okay and I was sick of going to the doctor every month. I wanted to try going back to work again. I was continually told by Aaron, mum, and my friends that I wasn't ready and that I should take more time. So, I went to the doctor for a new form and was planning on going back to work again in the next month. Usually, I would just call my regular GP and ask for a new form. She knew exactly what I needed, would print it off and I would just have to go pick it up from the desk. Only this time, I had to see a new doctor because mine was on maternity leave. The thought of talking to a stranger. The thought of having to explain my situation and why I was there, gave me extreme anxiety. Before Zoie, I was usually a very calm person. Nothing really bothered me, but this day, sitting in that waiting room, I was sweating. I was shaking. I dry reached. I closed my eyes. Calm down Karina and just breathe, I told myself. After that experience, I decided to listen to my friends and family and take some more time. After all, Zoie's birthday was coming up the next month and the month after that, was going to be the bus driver's court case.

I then found a new doctor that I felt comfortable with. She was thorough and gave extra attention to my mental health. I had made it through Zoie's birthday and the first court mention. Instead of breaking again, I felt I was staying strong. I was no longer stuck in a thick fog, being thrown around in the middle of the ocean. I was feeling a little like my old self again. I could socialise, be present in the moment and hold a conversation. I could focus and organise myself. I started making my follow-up appointments to see my breast cancer doctors that I had neglected for the past year. I became more aware of how some of the boys were struggling at school and organised help for them. But the biggest thing for me was that I now found joy in the simple things again. I was falling back in love with the Earth and nature. It filled me with pride and joy to watch my kids playing and laughing. I had fun with my friends and family again.

Before eight months, I was not ready. I wanted to be. I tried to be. I just wanted to pretend that life was back to normal as much as I could.

I finally returned to work almost 10 months after Zoie's death, on 20 April 2021. In the meantime, work had got a new care manager. I emailed her and arranged a time to go in and meet her to discuss my return to work. She was nice and approachable. She agreed with my request to only start back for four days a fortnight and not to do medications for a couple weeks until I found my feet again and got to know the residents. I said hello to a few work colleagues, renewed my computer passwords and briefly went over some resident profiles to get up to date while I was there. I felt comfortable and focused while there. Like I was back in my second home.

This time, being back at work, although Zoie was still constantly on my mind, I was not filled with pain. I was focused on my residents and the job at hand. I felt clear minded, comfortable and confident. I felt like my old self at work again.

I still had my bad days where I would second guess being back. Although I was only doing four days a fortnight, I still had to call in sick a couple of times, like on Mother's Day. That hit me like a ton of bricks, out of nowhere. Then the one-year anniversary came along. During the one month in the lead up to the anniversary, I became very edgy and very emotional. I missed Zoie with an unbearable force. I still don't know how, but I guess I just willed myself to push on and keep working. I wanted to move on. I wanted to live a normal and happy life, even if I had to fake it first.

I continued to work and became more and more comfortable and confident. I picked up an extra shift, doing five shifts a fortnight. I felt like life was back on track. That was until I was diagnosed with breast cancer again in August 2021. It was picked up in my regular, yearly mammogram. I was only back at work for five months before I had to stop again while I had chemotherapy and a mastectomy. I knew that place was cursed!

When I was diagnosed with breast cancer for the second time, my grief and longing to be with Zoie came back with a vengeance. I was thrown right back to day one again. I hit another low. I had just spent the last year battling my inner demons and had finally won. Now I was given another chance to be with Zoie. Treat the cancer and stay with my husband and the boys and likely live a long and happy life. Or don't treat the cancer and be with Zoie. At the time of diagnoses, I was on the path to happiness. I could see a glimmer of hope. Now it was like Zoie was holding open the door to heaven, waiting for me. She felt so close that I just had to take her outstretched hand. I simply had to opt for no treatment and quickly make my way to Zoie and that open door. If I opted for treatment, Zoie would shut the door, leaving her on the other side and me here with my whole family. I literally had to choose between my kids. Zoie or the boys? Do I go to Zoie, or do I stay here with my family? Either way, I lose someone. My decision came down to this; we had all already lost Zoie. I believe she can still see us. Zoie isn't missing a thing. Aaron and the boys didn't need to lose me too. Aaron and I still had plans to travel, see the boys graduate school, get married and give me grandbabies. I wanted to be here for all that. I had already lost Zoie's future. I didn't want to lose my future with the rest of my family. So, I told Zoie to shut the door and I would see her when it was my time.

I still feel passionately about aged care and nursing, but I need to focus on my health first. I can't look after others if I don't look after myself. I am fortunate enough to be financially able to take time off and survive with Aaron's wage until I am well enough to return.

diary

Thurs, 1/4/2021

Dear diary,

Last night was horrible. Aaron had to go to work early, at 8pm. I said good night to all the boys and sat up for another two hours and had a cuppa. Without Aaron home, who usually calms me in his presence, I was so noticeably alone and missing Zoie, wishing she was here.

I finally went to bed, with no Aaron to comfort me. I cried painful, chesty sobs that took my breath away.

Just before I fell asleep from pure exhaustion, the TV turned on all on its own as it has done several times since Zoie died. I got up, turned the TV off and said, 'Good night Zoie. I love you'. I went to bed, exhausted, but calm and went to sleep.

I then dreamed of Zoie. She was back from the dead again, telling me of the events that had happened while she was dead.

Thurs, 15/4/2021

Dear diary,

I have been slightly emotional all week leading up to the court case. I did a Facebook stalk to find a photo of the driver. I just had to know what he looks like. I wanted to prepare myself in case I saw him at court. I think this is what has stirred me up.

The bus driver did not show up at court today and his lawyer pleaded not guilty on his behalf. The case was adjourned until 27 May. We just wanted to see some remorse and accountability. To plead not guilty, when we had reason to believe he was, because it was on camera and in the driver's statement, that he did not stop at a stop sign, was a huge kick in the guts to us and told us that he was not remorseful at all. We are so angry.

People keep telling me how the driver is not coping well and has mental health issues because of the accident. Do they think I should feel sorry for him? Well, I don't. He should feel bad. I fully understand that it was an accident, but in my opinion that accident was caused by the driver's negligence, and he took my baby girl away from me. I have to live in pain and misery for the rest of my life, and so should he. I would have been happy for him to plead guilty, show a little remorse for what he had done and just get a fine for not stopping. I would have forgiven him. Now I hope he gets the full 18 months in prison.

Sun, 9/5/2021

Dear diary,

I had a rough day today with it being Mother's Day. Zoie was my first born. The one that made me a mum for the first time. Today is the first Mother's Day since becoming a mum, that I've had to spend without one of my babies. I cried almost as soon as I woke up and had to call in sick for work. I was a mess all day.

I started back at work on 20 April, for four days a fortnight. This time it feels right. I can think clearly and I am comfortable and confident at work. Last time, I was numb and in a fog and couldn't focus on anything. I am feeling good at work. I think I'm coming good again. I just hope it's not another 'calm before the storm'.

Thurs, 27/5/2021

Dear diary,

I saw the bus driver in Coles last week. I was standing behind someone else at the front service desk when I saw him at a register a few meters up from me. I did a double take, not sure if it was him at first. After studying his face for a moment, I realised that it was definitely him and froze in my spot. I turned away from him, hoping he didn't recognise me. I started to panic. Do I stay or do I run out the door? I stayed, finished what I had to do and got out as fast as I could.

The driver's second court mention was today. He didn't turn up again and the case was adjourned until 1 July, of all days. I am so angry and frustrated. I just want it finalised either way so that I can close this chapter.

16

THE COURT CASE

On Wednesday, 23 December, two days before our first Christmas without Zoie, we took the boys to the movies. It was the first real outing we had with the boys for the holidays since Zoie died. They didn't really have fun activities in the July or September school holidays. We had just left the movies when the police detective in charge of Zoie's case called and said that he needed to speak to Aaron and me urgently. We drove straight home and the detective met us there 15 minutes later. He informed us that the bus driver had been charged with two driving offences; negligent driving occasioning death, and failing to stop at a stop sign. The reason for the urgency was that it was going to be in the media. And it was. It was in the paper and posted all over Facebook the very next day.

Aaron and I were relieved. Finally, after almost six months, we had our closure. We didn't necessarily want the driver fined or jailed. All we wanted was for it to be noted that he was in the wrong by not stopping at the stop sign and for the driver to own responsibility for that. I wanted him to plead guilty and take responsibility for the pain and suffering he caused my family and me.

The court date was set for a mention on 15 April. I didn't know what that meant. I didn't know what to expect on the day. I was not familiar with court proceedings. All I did know is that I wanted remorse and a guilty plea from the driver.

Aaron and I attended the Milton Courthouse on 15 April 2021. The court officer approached us and asked me what case I was there for. I stated the driver's name. She asked what my relation to the matter was. My mind scattered. Oh, shit! What do I say? 'He is involved in my daughter's accident', I said. The court officer told me that the case was just a mention. The driver was not in attendance, but his lawyer was. She told us that the lawyer will make a plea on the driver's behalf, the case will be adjourned until a later date, and she would come and get me when it was time to go in.

I noticed a casually dressed man with a camera standing outside the courthouse. I immediately thought that he must be media and tried to hide my face from him so that I wouldn't be recognized and harassed. About half an hour later, I noticed a well-dressed man leave the court room with the man with the camera. At that moment, the court officer approach me again and apologized. She had been out the back and hadn't heard the case called. The court officer informed us that the case had just finished. The driver had made a 'not guilty plea' to negligent driving, guilty to not stopping at the stop sign, and the case was adjourned until 27 May.

Not guilty! Aaron and I were gutted, disappointed and furious with that plea. We just wanted some remorse and, to us, a not guilty plea was saying that the driver did not take accountability for what he had done. He did not stop at the stop sign. It was in his statement and on the bus cameras, so how could he say that he was not guilty to negligent driving. And why not show up at court if you are not guilty. I believe he was probably advised by his lawyer but, to me, not showing up and pleading not guilty was gutless and a huge kick in the guts to me and my family. There was no remorse. There was no accountability taken. And now we had to go through it all again in more mentions and a hearing. I was so angry.

Within two hours, the South Coast register paper contacted Shelly through the 'go fund me' page for a statement from me.

Someone from Nine news messaged me on Facebook to contact them. I was out at lunch with Aaron at the time, so I didn't reply. Half an hour later, he called my phone. How on Earth did he get my number? I thought. I spoke with him and agreed to give him a statement, but I stipulated that I did not want to appear on TV.

As predicted, the media covered the story repeatedly over the next two days. Aaron and I camped out on Shelly's property for the weekend, staying away from the TV and radio.

~

The second mention was held on 27 May 2021. Again, Aaron and I went to the courthouse. Again, the driver did not show. There was no media presence this time and I had no phone calls from them. There was nothing on Facebook or in the newspapers. The court official told us the outcome of the case. The case was adjourned for a third mention five weeks later, which fell on the one-year anniversary of Zoie's death.

I was so annoyed. I just wanted the case to go to a hearing.

To get it over and done with and close that chapter. As hard as I tried, I couldn't get the court case out of my head until it was over. I think I was anxious to know if the case would go to trial, if the driver was found guilty or not, and what his sentence would be, if anything.

~

The third mention was on the 1 July 2021, the one year anniversary of Zoie's death. We didn't go to the court for that because it was going to be for us and to be all about Zoie, our grief and what we had lost. It was not going to be about the driver. He had taken our princess from us; he was not going to have that day too.

It was on our minds, though. I had to know what happened, so I called the charging police detective and asked him. He came around the next day to tell Aaron and me in person that the case would be going ahead to a hearing in Nowra Court on 14 December 2021. It would now be up to the judge to decide if the bus driver's actions were negligent.

In my opinion, it is negligent driving to not come to a complete stop at a stop sign, in a school zone, as a school bus driver. So yes, I wanted him to get the maximum penalty, which is only 18 months in prison. Why should he be able to go home, see his family every day and enjoy his children and grandchildren when I never get to see my little princess grow up to be an adult? Or see her get married. I won't have grandchildren from my only daughter, all because he didn't want to wait a few more seconds.

I was so happy that it wasn't on hold again for another mention. It was finally coming to an end. On the morning of the hearing, I was so nervous. The thought of seeing the driver made me nauseous. As the hearing date got closer, I was not angry at the driver anymore. I didn't care what his sentencing would be, I just wanted to see his remorse and have it noted that he was in the wrong. One way or another, I just wanted the court case to be over, to know the verdict and close this torturous chapter.

As I sat out the front of the courthouse on a cold steel bench seat, with Aaron, Shelly, and Aaron's sister for support, I noticed a group of people standing out the front of a building across the road. It was the driver, his family and his solicitor. The family constantly looked over in my direction with a look of disgust and disappointment on their faces. In hindsight, they were probably just curious, anxious and as nervous as I was but, at the time, I felt so judged. As soon as I saw his face, I knew it was the driver. I studied his face and demeanor from a distance, trying to catch a glimpse or feeling of remorse from him, but all I got was arrogance. I watched him as he walked past me in and out of the court room, waiting for him to make eye contact with me. He never did. To be honest, I was so nervous about seeing him and had no idea what I would have said or done if he had made eye contact or said anything. I probably would have stood frozen on the spot like a deer in head lights.

I was continually asked by the charging officer if I wanted to stay in the court room and warned about the graphic video images I would see. I wanted to see and hear everything. I had to know if the images I had running constantly through my head for the past seventeen months were exactly what had happened.

I was not shocked or surprised by anything I heard or saw in the hearing because I had already asked the police and witnesses several questions and pieced the whole accident together. I had visualized the whole thing in detail in my mind over and over again for seventeen months. When I watched the video footage in court, it was like I was watching the same horror movie I knew so well. It was exactly what had been playing in my mind.

The driver's defence was the traffic and road conditions and the blind spot on the bus created by the bus's left side mirror caused the driver to not be able to see Zoie. They argued that the stop sign had been moved forward three meters following the accident. There were new line markings on the side of St Vincent Street (where Zoie was hit) following the accident, clearly showing a no stopping, parking or driving area.

The prosecution argued that the accident could have been avoided if the driver had stopped at the stop line.

Both sides presented evidence including CCTV footage, surveys of the road, crash investigation specialist, and witness statements. No witnesses had to be present in court, as their statements were enough and presented to the magistrate. I was so happy that they didn't have to relive it all again, as some of the witnesses were close friends of Zoie's. I felt the hearing went well and in our favour. The bus cameras and a car dash cam clearly showed the bus did not stop at the stop sign. Although it was not clear as to where Zoie was looking, the video footages also showed Zoie standing on the curb waiting while a black ute in front of the bus turned left and drove past her. Zoie then stepped out onto the road as the bus rolled through the stop sign following the ute. The footage showed the left side of the bus collide with Zoie.

The case was set for yet another mention on 4 February 2022, to allow both sides to present all their evidence and statements to the magistrate to look over properly. I understood and agreed with the reason for another mention, but I was so frustrated to have to wait even longer. I just wanted it over and done with.

The verdict was originally set for 14 March 2022, but as Aaron and I arrived at the courthouse, the charging officer informed us that the magistrate's husband had covid meaning she was a close contact and couldn't attend court, so it was put over to April 6, 2022.

Finally, 21 months after Zoie's death, on Wednesday April 6 was verdict day. Of all court days, this was the one I really wanted to be there for. This was the one that mattered. I got covid, testing positive the day before so Aaron and I were unable to attend but we had family go in our place. I felt I needed someone to be there for Zoie. I tried calling the charging officer the day before and the morning of court, but I was unable to get hold of him. I left a text and voice message explaining that I wouldn't be there for the verdict and wanted to know if it was possible to be on the phone or zoom call for the verdict, but he was on leave and I didn't hear back from him till a week later.

Court started 9:30am. I sat by my phone and waited anxiously for any news. Mum called me at 10am as she was leaving court and gave me the verdict.

All charges dismissed! The magistrate dismissed most of the video footage as they did not clearly show Zoie. The magistrate accepted a witness statement stating that Zoie did not look both ways before stepping off the curb. The magistrate acknowledged that the driver did not stop at the stop sign before stating the driver acted like a reasonable and prudent person and his actions did not contribute to Zoie's death. The magistrate stated that the driver had a clean driving record and had suffered significant mental health issues as a result of the accident and the driver was placed on a nine-month conditional release order.

I broke down in tears as soon as I heard the outcome. I was shattered and felt my grief just as raw as I had the day Zoie died. I cried all day to the point it was hard to breathe, and it felt like my chest was being ripped open. As I cooked dinner with a wet face filled with tears, sucking in sobbing breaths, all I was thinking is how we are here hurting, grieving Zoie no longer being here with us, looking at her bedroom door that she will never walk out of again and her empty spot at the dinner table she will never sit at again, all while thinking how the bus driver and his family are all probably having the happiest dinner they have had in 21 months and celebrating that they can now get on with their lives happily ever after.

17

HOW I'VE CHANGED

I used to be a calm, happy and positive person. Nothing ever really bothered me. I wasn't easily stressed. I had no issue being in social situations. I changed in many ways after losing Zoie. I became anxious when I left my home. I was fearful of the boys crossing any road. I used to love life and being out in nature. Now I am content to stay at home and indulge in Netflix series or read a book, just to escape my reality. Grief consumed every minute of every day, and I didn't believe I would ever feel happiness again.

Sleep changes

I have always needed a solid eight hours sleep each night and an extra hour or two sleep-in on the weekends never hurt. Before Zoie, I didn't have any problems with my sleep. I would go to bed at around 11pm, fall asleep easily and wake about 7am. Now, for some God-forsaken reason, I often wake at 3am when Aaron goes to work and can't go back to sleep for hours.

I have always been a dreamer, but I had never had a bad dream or nightmare. A year after Zoie died, I began having bad dreams that would wake me up. My heart would be pounding and I'd be unable to get back to sleep.

These days, I am always tired. Not the sort of tired that sleep can satisfy, but the deeper kind. A soulful fatigue that needs much more than rest.

Anxiety

Before Zoie's death, I had always been a calm, confident and independent person. Nothing ever really bothered me. I was very rarely stressed. After Zoie died, I didn't want to leave my house, partly because I felt closer to Zoie at home, but I also would get paranoid that people would see me and gossip about me. I was worried that I would be judged for being out and about and accused of moving on so quickly. I was worried I'd run into someone I knew and be asked how I am and feared that I would break down in public.

I wanted to return to work, but worried that I wouldn't be able to focus or manage the extra workload on top of my home duties and felt I was a failure if I couldn't do both.

All this stress took a toll on my body. I often had diarrhea. My skin would break out in pimples and I had an irritated throat like there was something stuck in there. This caused coughing attacks and sometimes I had trouble swallowing food. I had many doctor appointments and tests, and it all came down to stress.

Not wanting to socialize

I was worried about how I would be perceived while I was out socializing because I had Zoie on my mind 24/7 and couldn't think or talk about anything else. I couldn't hold an interesting conversation. I was sad and depressed. I was not in the mood to socialize and have a good time. I was not okay and, for a long time, I didn't want to be okay. I missed Zoie and I wanted her back. I also feared being judged if I dared to have a good time. I felt guilty if I did smile or laugh.

Lack of patience

I used to be a good listener. Friends would come to me with their day-to-day dramas that now seemed so petty. I liked being that person. I liked offering my calm, resilient advice. Now I have very little patience for petty dramas and issues.

There are times when everyone wants help with something all at the one time. Parents want help connecting internet to their TV. Friends complain about their inattentive partners or shitty, annoying kids. People asked me to run errands for them. My kids were constantly at me, 'Mum, can I have. Mum, can I get. Mum, what's for dinner? Mum, I'm bored'. My mind would be so overloaded that it would all just get too much and I would shut down. Being the introverted person I am, I would need to get away on my own for a while. Even just half an hour a day. Quiet, with no one else around. I'd meditate or go for a walk up the beach. Or just clean the house while I blast some music and sung at the top of my lungs with tears streaming down my face.

18

1 YEAR ANNIVERSARY

As the one-year anniversary approached, I became more and more edgy again. Memories of being told the news by the police would come back to me. That conversation would roll over and over in my head. I would have tears threatening to fall all day, every day for a whole month in the lead up to the 1st. It got harder and harder to pretend to be okay.

I started to question if I really wanted to be back at work because I didn't really want to leave the house. Again, I started to withdraw and self-isolate. But I didn't want to just give up on work again either. I had to push and remind myself that I never used to like being a stay-at-home mum. I have always wanted to have my own identity, other than 'being a mum'. I want to feel like I am contributing financially to our family. I might always have days like this, so I need to work through it.

The night before the first anniversary, I was rostered on to work. I felt emotionally okay, emotionally strong. About an hour before I had to leave for work, stupid me wanting to be prepared, so I read out to Aaron a speech I had prepared for the next day. I cried the whole way through it and stirred up my emotions for the afternoon. When I arrived at work, everyone was asking me how I was in a way that made it clear they all knew that the next day was the anniversary. I was holding back tears for the whole seven-hour shift. I was able to talk briefly with work colleagues about the pending day, but would cut conversations short, making excuses to keep moving when I started to feel the lump in my throat and tears build.

The hardest to take was one resident who would repeatedly ask, 'Is it Thursday, the 1st of July in the morning?' And I would respond that it was. Each time she asked, I could picture Zoie and the lump in my throat would return, accompanied by the crushing pain in my chest. I just wanted to bang my head against the brick wall.

'Yes love, it is Thursday, the 1st, tomorrow', I would answer in the sweetest voice I could manage with a smile on my face. I would just have to walk away from her, while screaming on the inside, I know what fucking day it is woman. Please just shut up!

Thursday, 1 July 2021 was the one-year anniversary and also the bus driver's third mention at court. That day was about Zoie's death, acknowledging and accepting it. I wanted to make it all about Zoie, not the bus driver that took her from me. I was not going to spend that morning at court. My emotions were bouncing around like popcorn. I cried all day, on and off almost from the moment I woke up. I felt like I'd been thrown back a year. My grief and pain were the same as when I was first told.

For the 1st anniversary, Aaron, the boys and I, along with some close family, all went out to our favorite camping spot. I felt like I had to make up for not speaking at Zoie's funeral, so I read a speech that I had prepared for this day. I cried the whole way through it. I had to pause a couple of times to breathe, but I am happy to say that I did it. I was able to say my proper goodbye. Then, one by one, we took turns scattering Zoie's ashes in the river, followed by a picnic lunch, where we sat amongst nothing but nature. Listening to the birds and the running river, it was beautiful and peaceful.

After lunch, we packed up and headed home to freshen up before heading down to the corner of Zoie's accident, where we had arranged to meet with friends and family, including Zoie's friends. Everyone placed some flowers on the fence and drew on the road with chalk. We wrote Zoie's name, messages to Zoie and drew butterflies and rainbows.

That whole section of road was blocked off because the council had finally started the pedestrian crossing on St Vincent Street. I thought this may have been an inconvenience, but it worked perfectly in our favour. It was like it had been blocked off just for us. We were all able to spread out all over the road and draw and chat.

After a little drawing and mingling, I sat on the road in the exact spot Zoie had died, watching everyone come together. Jacob and Tyson sat with me, cuddling into me from either side as I cried. I was shaking, had a lump in my throat and a knot in my stomach. I was in so much pain. I miss having a daughter, another girl in the house. I miss Zoie. There I was surrounded by people that love and support me, Aaron and the boys, and yet I felt lost, empty and broken. I just wanted Zoie back.

I was completely exhausted for the next two days.

At the end of the day, I had a bottle of wine and cried for hours. I messaged the charging police officer, to ask for any updates on what had happened at court. The officer came around to our house the following day to inform us that the bus driver's next court day was a hearing in Nowra on 14 December 2021. Aaron and I were happy and relieved that it wasn't being put off again with another mention.

Sat, 5/6/2021

Dear diary,

I have been tired, emotional and not sleeping well all week. I think I am going downhill in the lead up to Zoie's one year anniversary. I try to push sad feelings to the back of my mind, but it is getting harder and harder to do.

I had an emotional day last Wednesday and had to call in sick for work. That plays on my mind too because I hate being unreliable. I'm considering taking this month off work, or do I just suck it up?

Fri, 2/7/2021

Dear diary,

I'm still exhausted after crying all day yesterday. I woke up and instantly cried uncontrollably. I wrapped my arms tightly around myself as I sobbed and struggled to breathe. I still feel like I have gone back a year.

I messaged the charging officer last night to see if he had an update on court yesterday. He came around today to tell us the that the driver's next court day will be a hearing on 14 December. We are so happy and relieved that it hasn't been put off again for another mention.

19

OPENING UP

Making small talk when meeting someone new is difficult. I would always dread the inevitable question that I knew was coming. It always does because it is a common conversation starter.

Do you have kids?

I am very open and honest with everyone about losing Zoie and I have no issues talking about Zoie, but for some reason, when I'm asked how many kids I have, I freeze.

Before Zoie, I would proudly say, 'Yes, five'. Which was always followed by, 'Boys or girls?' 'Four boys and one girl', I would proudly say. That would always lead to more questions about Zoie. 'Oh, only girl, she must be tough with four brothers! Or is she spoilt?'

Then I would have to explain my situation or talk about Zoie as if she was still here.

The first time I was asked this question after Zoie died, I replied, 'Yeah, I have four boys'. I felt terrible and so guilty. What about Zoie? I still have a daughter and I can't just pretend she never existed. But how do I explain to a stranger that I have a daughter, but she died. I don't want to have that depressive conversation every time I meet someone new.

I still feel like I have a daughter. I do still have a daughter and I must acknowledge her always. So, now I will reply, 'Yes, I have five. Four boys and a daughter in spirit'. The good thing about living in my small town is that most people I meet already know who I am and about Zoie, so I don't have to explain often.

I am open and honest about my grief and losing Zoie when I am asked about it, but sometimes I think it is too much for people to hear.

When I'm asked how I am, I now reply, 'I'm okay'. It is just easier to lie. Easier for everyone else, but not for me. The truth is, I hated life. My world seemed dark and miserable. I didn't enjoy any aspect of it. I often thought of suicide. It wasn't that I wanted to die, but that was literally the only way I could see Zoie any time soon and being with Zoie was all I could think about. I look forward to the day I walk through the pearly gates and it saddens me to think that I more than likely have decades to wait.

Sometimes, I didn't know how I felt. I couldn't articulate it. I felt numb, angry, empty, sad, love and everything else in between, all at once.

I am now a different Karina from who I was before losing Zoie. I am still getting to know and understand her. I am filled with anxiety, guilt and sadness every day. I am unmotivated to work. I am not interested in socializing. I miss having a daughter. I miss Zoie with every inch of my being.

People can't understand the depth of my pain. They don't want to acknowledge it. They just want to fix it. To make me feel better.

People would be lost for words or feel bad for asking how I am, like they had just reminded me of my pain. It got to a point where I stopped being so honest. I didn't open up to many people because they couldn't understand my pain or handle hearing how bad I really was. It was just easier to say, 'Yeah, I'm okay'.

At times, I was okay and could begin to talk openly again about my heartbreaking story, like it was an everyday thing. I would then be confronted with sorrow and empathy. This brought me back to the reality that I really did have a rough time. Am I that messed up that I have simply accepted that this pain and misery is normal? Or am I just not ashamed of what I have been through and how I managed it? Maybe I have started to believe my own lies. Believing that I'm okay. Maybe bereaved parents should talk openly about it more to normalize the conversations so that other people don't feel awkward talking about it.

My battles are often now the quiet ones no one knows about. They see what I want them to see. Behind closed doors and silent tears, I cry from inexplicable sadness, momentary frustration and an absolute longing to see my girl.

I don't seek pity. I am strong. Not by choice, but because being strong is my only choice. I don't see it as being strong. I see it as surviving. I go about my days now, much as I used to, trying to be a good, loving and nurturing mum, and an attentive and devoted wife. Only now, there is a big, dark cloud on my shoulder every minute of every day. I unwillingly carry it around with me, trying to ignore the all-consuming pain that comes with it.

20

DREAMS OF ZOIE

I often dream of Zoie. They are always about the time after her death, and she has come back to me in one way or another. She has either come back from the dead or she wasn't actually dead but had just run away. I talk to her. I hug her. She talks to me about her death and the effects it's had on her friends and family.

Dreams of Zoie are bittersweet because they are so vivid. While it is amazing to be able to see and talk to my baby girl in my dreams, these dreams always send me back to day one. I wake up feeling like I have lost Zoie all over again. I get a heavy chest and I struggle to breathe. I feel like I was just with her. She was sitting right next to me. Now, when I look, she's not there. My heart breaks all over again.

I want so badly to go back to sleep so that I can be with my girl again, but no matter how hard I try, I can never get back to sleep after these dreams. I am left heartbroken with tears constantly falling all day, while I try unsuccessfully to pull myself together.

The friends

I only had all boys at home now. I missed Zoie. I missed having a daughter. A daughter who would tell me all about her day, her friends. Who had a crush on who? Who was fighting with whom? What was happening at school? I was looking forward to dress shopping for her year 10 formal. The boys just don't talk about this stuff. It's hard to get any information out of them.

When Zoie died, I didn't just lose Zoie, I lost her friends as well. I wanted to stay close to those girls. I guess, in a way, I was wanting to experience what Zoie's life would have been like, vicariously, through her friends. I could be kept up to date on school things, like the formal and see all the girl's dresses. I could watch them grow into adults, as they graduated, got jobs, travelled, got married and had kids.

For this reason, I stayed in touch with a few of Zoie's closest friends through social media. I invited them to Zoie's birthday and anniversary each year.

I bought a Pandora bangle in 2020 that I would have given to Zoie for that Christmas had she still been here. It just sat unworn in my jewellery box for a year after Zoie died. I wanted it to go to someone special. I gave it to one of 11 of Zoie's closes friends, with instructions to pass it on to the next girl on the first of every month.

I have always liked Zoie's friends. She had a great choice of friends and chose them wisely. Although I knew of them all and was pleased with Zoie's circle of friends, I didn't know all of them personally. Almost instantly after Zoie died, I felt a strong connection with her friends. The way I describe the feeling is that it's like I now feel Zoie's love and connection to her friends for her, just as she did.

I treasure 'Zoie's girls', as I call them, and wanted to stay in touch with them. I guess that's why I invite them all to Zoie's birthday celebrations and anniversaries.

It is also the reason behind the bangle. I guess it keeps me in touch with the girls, but also keeps a connection between them.

21

MOVING ON

So, how did I get through it? Well, I just didn't give up although there were many times that I wanted to, I kept on going for my family. I spoke openly to everyone all the time about my grief. I speak to Zoie often still. Sometimes out loud, sometimes in my head as a prayer. I feel Zoie is still here in spirit, connected to my soul. That might make me sound crazy, but I'm okay with that. Zoie is still my daughter. She is still a part of my life and I won't ignore her just because I can't see her. I rested when I needed rest. Some days all I could do was breathe. What helped me most was Charmaine Wilson. She helped me to understand the spirit world. Through Charmaine, I was able to accept death as a natural part of life. I was able to accept that Zoie died when she did because it was just her time.

For the first six months, I didn't see any light. There was no hope for better days. I thought my future was inevitably dark and miserable. Only after time, did that darkness fade. It is still there, only now I am not consumed by it. It follows me around like a rain cloud hovering over my head.

People often tell me that I am strong, inspirational and that I should be proud. I don't feel strong or proud. I feel like I have been shoved into a new universe like Alice in Wonderland. I don't know if I'm trying to survive like an alien on a strange planet that I can't breathe on, or if I'm just lost and trying to find my way home.

There are many mornings where I stand in the shower just letting the almost-scolding hot water wash over me. Head down, I pray to a god I'm not even sure I believe in, to help me muster up the strength for my day, and vaguely hope the water will wash away some of my pain.

This is what people don't see, that I have days that take everything I have left in me, just to show up. Because everyone sees the smile on my face and positive attitude and just assumes that I am a strong, inspirational and unbreakable woman. The truth is, though, I break more often than I don't. I just don't always show my pain to the people around me.

The boys need me to be strong, to be smiling and have fun, to keep going, no matter what. That takes a toll on me some days. I cry for a few minutes when I'm in the shower or sit in the car an extra few minutes in the driveway, just staring and searching for a bit more strength to push ahead.

I lie in bed every night, utterly spent from my day and pray that I find a way to keep going when my soul is weary. Every fibre in my being is exhausted, yet I know sleep won't help. What I need is to be with my daughter. I don't ask for help. I know there is no help. No cure. It is just something I have to go through.

It is not that I want to be strong, or that I chose to be a fighter. My life never gave me any other choice. So now, I do what I have to do. Sometimes with a worrier spirit conquering the world, and other times, squeezing out every bit of energy to pull myself through the day. Even when I am holding back tears, I still force a smile and say, 'I'm okay', because I know it's okay to not be okay.

I couldn't control what life threw my way, but I could control how I responded, how long I stay depressed and suffered. I needed to take the time to grieve, to be sad, but then I had to make the choice to get up, move forward and live again. I knew that Zoie would want me to find joy and happiness. Her spirit is with me every day. She would not want to hang out with me, being sad and miserable.

I didn't have any expectations for myself. I had no goal. I just took each day as it came. I felt the highs and I rode the lows. I didn't ignore any of my feelings. When I felt down and out, I would rest at home, usually crying. When I felt strong, I pushed for normality and kept busy.

What helped me get through each day was:

- Going to the gym, to move all the built-up grief.
- Making the choice to want to move on and be happy.
- Aaron and having a great support network.
- Charmaine Wilson and understanding the spirit world.

I have to believe that I will see Zoie again when my time on Earth comes to an end. Believing I will one day see my princess again, is what keeps me going.

diary

Mon, 1/11/21

Dear diary,
One of Zoie's best friend's, Izzy. got me again today. I saw her at the Halloween fundraiser last night that the lolly shop held for us. I was randomly thinking of her being there and tears built up in my eyes. The same thing happened when Izzy messaged me to say that she had the bangle. I instantly cried and felt so happy that she had it. It is like I have this weird connection to Izzy. Whenever I think of her, it's like Zoie is somehow connected to that thought or to Izzy.

Tues, 21/12/21

Dear diary,
It is coming up to 18 months since Zoie died. In four days, we will have our second Christmas without her and bring in yet another new year. It doesn't feel like Christmas. I just can't seem to feel the festive spirit. I have the Christmas tree up, decorations all around and watch Christmas movies. It all seems forced. Still, I look forward to having Christmas Day with Aaron's side of the family. The boys are all excited for Christmas and that's the main thing. The boys are why I make an effort to continue normality and traditions.

I often wonder what Zoie would look like now and how she may have changed. I hate the fact that I have adjusted to life without her. I guess, in a way, I still feel like she has moved interstate or even overseas and I have just accepted that she won't be coming home to visit.

I took the kids to the beach today. I have missed the beach. Either the weather has not been favorable, or I have been sick from chemo, but today, although I was not feeling the best this morning, it was a perfect, hot summer day, so I forced myself to freshen up and go. I'm so glad I did now. The water was lovely and refreshing. Watching the boys smiling, laughing and jumping through the waves, filled me with joy, temporarily removing me from my self-pity and feeling sick.

Wed, 6/4/22

Dear diary,

What the fuck have I done to deserve to be continually knocked down time and time again over the last 21 months. Zoie walks into a bus and is killed, I get diagnosed with HER2 positive breast cancer, endure chemotherapy, have a mastectomy, need to wait over a year for a breast reconstruction, I get Covid and have to miss verdict day in court, and the bus driver gets all charges dropped.

Today was verdict day at court. Me Aaron and Tyson have covid, tested positive yesterday so we are all in isolation and couldn't attend. Mum, Noel, April, and Shelly went for us.

The magistrate dismissed all charges, and the driver was let off with a nine-month conditional release order. She said the drivers' actions didn't contribute to Zoie's death after acknowledging he didn't stop at the stop sign. He didn't even get a fine for not stopping.

The charging officer wasn't there, and I haven't been able to contact him before or after court. I thought being the charging officer, he would have to be there.

I am shattered. I am back to day 1 grief and so angry he got nothing. I broke down in tears as soon as I was told the verdict over the phone by mum as she was leaving the court. I cried all day to the point it was hard to breathe. I feel like my chest is being ripped open. As I cooked dinner with a wet face filled with tears and sucking in sobbing breaths all I was thinking is how we are here hurting, grieving Zoie no longer being here with us, looking at her bedroom door that she will never walk out of again and her empty spot at the dinner table she will never sit at again, all while thinking how the bus driver and his family are all probably having the happiest dinner they have had in 21 months and celebrating that they can now get on with their lives happily ever after.

It was so formal; there was no mention or concern for me or my family by the court; It is like the driver is the victim, and Zoie just another death statistic.

I had a dream last night that we all went to court for verdict day. It was a massive court room and I got separated from everyone else going in. I sat next to a toddler that was wearing the same pants Zoie used to have as a toddler. Then it was like I saw young Zoie in a fleeting thought, and she told me the case was going to be dismissed, and that was the end of the dream.

22

LIFE WITHOUT ZOIE

There is no denying that I changed dramatically after losing Zoie. It took a toll on my mind, body and spirit. I went from being a happy, carefree, positive person to a negative and depressed person. I fought daily with my inner demons and saw no hope of happiness again. Only after some time, did the light start to shine back into life. First, I had to take the time to adjust to my grief. I had to adjust to life without Zoie. I had to take time to heal. To focus on me, one day at a time. Finally, I came to accept that this is my life. This did happen and there is nothing I can do to change it. I may not always be able to control my emotions, but what I can control are my thoughts and how I live my life. I made the choice to live a happy, positive life again for Zoie and for my family.

Sixteen months after Zoie's death, I was no longer angry at the driver. Being angry will not bring Zoie back, and it certainly doesn't make me feel any better. I decided to forgive the driver, even if I never saw remorse or heard an apology from him. I forgave him for me, not for him. Forgiving him, to me, meant letting go of the bitterness I felt towards him. Forgiveness allowed me to live again. To feel love, peace and joy.

Grief still pops in to rear its ugly head occasionally, on special occasions or when I am reminded of my pain. Although it will never fully go away for good, my grief no longer consumes me day in and day out.

Zoie always has and always will occupy such a huge part of my heart and soul. I talk about her because I am proud of my daughter. I talk about her because Zoie deserves to be remembered. I talk about Zoie because, even though she is not physically with me, she is always in my heart and on my mind. Zoie is a part of me, a part I could never ignore or disown.

Her spirit lives on in all the love and memories she left us with. I still have a relationship with Zoie, only now it is a spiritual one, not physical. I feel a connection to Zoie's soul and no amount of time or distance can break that.

Nowadays, I can socialize, laugh and have a good time without feeling guilty. I once again find joy in the simple things in life. I enjoy playing with my boys and watching them laughing, smiling and having fun. I see the beauty in the sun, the moon and nature. I feel peace and even happiness knowing that every time I am having fun, Zoie is right there enjoying it with me.

If you are a newly bereaved parent, you won't think it is possible to feel happiness again. I didn't either, but trust me, if you allow yourself to, you can and will be happy again.

There is no time limit on grief, but there is a time limit on life, so don't waste it being depressed. Yes, losing a child is unbearable and you will feel shit for a while, but don't chase happiness like it is a destination. Happiness is a feeling. Just like sadness, anger and excitement. You can't always be happy. Life will always throw us curve balls. Sometimes life just sucks. It's okay to have a bad day, week, or month, but that doesn't mean you have a bad life!

At the end of each day, write down a 'to do' list for the next day. Even if it is just two or three things. It can be small things like going for a walk along the beach, having coffee with a friend, baking a cake or vacuuming. You may not feel like getting up in the morning, but if you push yourself to complete your list, you will feel accomplished.

Make a time each day to grieve. To cry. To be angry. Then shower, get dressed and do something that does or used to make you happy. This helped me to get up each day. Eventually, I started to notice things that made me smile or laugh.

These days, I like to try and find a positive in every situation. A silver lining. Within one year after Zoie's accident, there were changes made to the roads around our local schools.

There is now a pedestrian crossing on the east side of the high school, St Vincent Street, about 50 meters from where Zoie was hit. There is council approval for traffic lights on that corner and another pedestrian crossing on the other side of the school in Camden Street to be commenced in the near future.

We now also have a crossing supervisor at the Milton Public School crossing. It makes me so happy to stop every morning for school children to cross the road at the new crossing. I say a silent prayer to Zoie, saying 'This is all because of you, my girl'. In a tragic, life-shattering way, Zoie helped bring road safety to our local schools.

I had always wanted to take all the kids to the Gold Coast in Queensland for a family holiday. I wanted to take them to all the big theme parks. I put it off for years because I wanted the kids to be old enough to remember it. We finally took this family holiday in October 2019. It was the best family holiday we have ever had. The kids loved it. Nine months later, Zoie died. I now have a new outlook on life. Not only Zoie's death, but my second cancer diagnosis really rattled me. It made me appreciate what I have and helped me to re-evaluate what is important in life. We are not guaranteed tomorrow, so I don't intend to waste my time putting things off for another day.

My aspiration in telling my story is to give newly bereaved parents hope for the future. There is no right or wrong way to grieve. In the first six to 12 months, you are going to experience heavy grief. Find whatever works for you. Some like to busy themselves with work. Maybe you might like to escape your reality and read books. Maybe you might join a boxing class. Take each day, one day at a time, and just breathe.

1. Riley, Tyson, Aaron, Jacob, Me, Zoie, Charlie

2. Family dinner at mums

3. Kids going for a ride in the ute

4. Zoie jumping off the rock

5. Zoie, Tyson, Riley, Jack, Jacob, Noah, Charlie

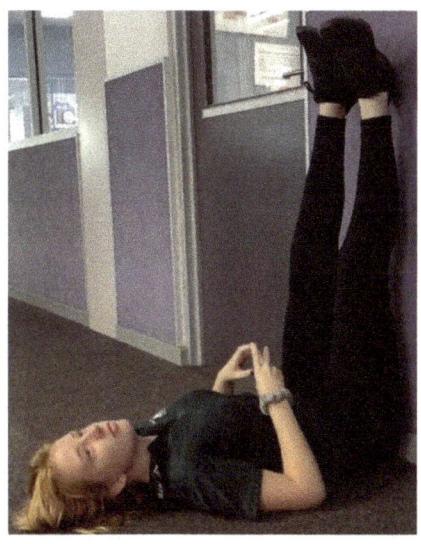

Zoie's 13th birthday

Zoie's girls

One year anniversary

ABOUT THE AUTHOR

Karina Adams, wife, and mother of five, was raised in Ulladulla on the NSW south coast. Karina considers her family to be most important to her. If she isn't spending time with her friends and family, at the beach with her two dogs or camping, you can almost always find her reading or writing.

Karina has battled breast cancer twice, enduring a lumpectomy, radiotherapy, chemotherapy, and a mastectomy by the age of 35.

After her daughter Zoie was hit and killed in a school bus accident, Karina began writing Losing Zoie as a form of therapy. This sparked Karina's passion for writing and publishing books.

www.ingramcontent.com/pod-product-compliance
Lightning Source LLC
Chambersburg PA
CBHW040742020526
44107CB00084B/2842